Fisher Investments on
Consumer Staples

FISHER INVESTMENTS PRESS

Fisher Investments Press brings the research, analysis, and market intelligence of Fisher Investments' research team, headed by CEO and *New York Times* best-selling author Ken Fisher, to all investors. The Press covers a range of investing and market-related topics for a wide audience—from novices to enthusiasts to professionals.

Books by Ken Fisher
The Ten Roads to Riches
The Only Three Questions That Count
100 Minds That Made the Market
The Wall Street Waltz
Super Stocks

Fisher Investments Series
Own the World
Aaron Anderson

20/20 Money
Michael Hanson

Fisher Investments On Series
Fisher Investments on Energy
Fisher Investments on Materials
Fisher Investments on Consumer Staples

FISHER
INVESTMENTS
PRESS

Fisher Investments on Consumer Staples

Fisher Investments
with
Michael Cannivet and
Andrew S. Teufel

WILEY

John Wiley & Sons, Inc.

Published by John Wiley & Sons, Inc., Hoboken, New Jersey.

Published simultaneously in Canada.

Important Disclaimers: This book reflects personal opinions, viewpoints, and analyses of the author and should not be regarded as a description of advisory services provided by Fisher Investments or performance returns of any Fisher Investments client. Fisher Investments manages its clients' accounts using a variety of investment techniques and strategies not necessarily discussed in this book. Nothing in this book constitutes investment advice or any recommendation with respect to a particular country, sector, industry, security, or portfolio of securities. All information is impersonal and not tailored to the circumstances or investment needs of any specific person.

Limit of Liability/Disclaimer of Warranty: While the publisher and author have used their best efforts in preparing this book, they make no representations or warranties with respect to the accuracy or completeness of the contents of this book and specifically disclaim any implied warranties of merchantability or fitness for a particular purpose. No warranty may be created or extended by sales representatives or written sales materials. Neither the publisher nor author shall be liable for any loss of profit or any other commercial damages, including but not limited to special, incidental, consequential, or other damages.

For general information on our other products and services or for technical support, please contact our Customer Care Department within the United States at (800) 762-2974, outside the United States at (317) 572-3993, or fax (317) 572-4002.

Wiley also publishes its books in a variety of electronic formats. Some content that appears in print may not be available in electronic books. For more information about Wiley products, visit our web site at www.wiley.com.

Library of Congress Cataloging-in-Publication Data:

Fisher Investments.

    Fisher Investments on consumer staples / Fisher Investments with Michael Cannivet, Andrew S. Teufel.

       p. cm. — (Fisher Investments Press)

    Includes bibliographical references and index.

    ISBN 978-0-470-41665-5

      1. Consumer goods—United States—History. 2. Consumption (Economics)—United States—History. I. Cannivet, Michael. II. Teufel, Andrew S. III. Title.

HF1040.8.F56 2009

332.67'22—dc22

    2009001913

Printed in the United States of America

10 9 8 7 6 5 4 3 2 1

Contents

Foreword

You're holding the third in a series of investing guides from Fisher Investments Press—the first ever imprint from a money management firm, produced in partnership with John Wiley & Sons. These guides are your introduction to a usable, top-down strategy for analyzing standard investing sectors (Energy, Materials, Consumer Staples, Health Care, Industrials, etc.) as well as other investing regions and categories. We plan on tackling them all.

Why publish an investing series when, to my knowledge, no other money manager has done it? Simple: It's a logical extension of standard operating procedure at my firm. We place a heavy premium on education—of our clients, of the broader world, and internally of our own employees who we work hard to promote internally. The more we teach, the more we can learn about capital markets, and the faster we can advance our own and others' understanding of how they work. This can only make us all better investors over time.

Consumer Staples is perhaps an underappreciated sector. It's not seen as hot and high growth—but this is a mistake. First, Consumer Staples has both growth and value areas—unusual but not unheard of for an investing sector. Second, it's wrong to think one sector is inherently better or worse than another. Given enough time, finance theory says all investing categories should net pretty similar returns when properly accounted for—though traveling different paths. Consumer Staples is no exception.

Consumer Staples plays a key role for global, top-down investors. Because there's generally inelastic demand for Staples goods and services, it's historically been a defensive play. This sector tends to hold up relatively well in market downturns, while generally lagging during boom times—but not always! A good investor needs to understand when and why Staples are likelier to lead or lag. Even if you believe Staples are apt to lag, they can still diversify and be a critical counter strategy should your bullish core strategy bets go awry. You'll read more on this in Chapter 7.

An interesting feature about Consumer Staples: Emerging markets goad demand for Staples products. (Though whether individual emerging markets emerge or submerge is a separate question entirely, one another impending Fisher Investments Press title, *Fisher Investments on Emerging Markets,* aims to answer.) Currently, in many less-developed economies, demand for Staples is more elastic, meaning the sector there can act more like its cousin, Consumer Discretionary. A good investor must know how and why that happens to make better, forward-looking overall forecasts. This book can teach you how.

Don't look to this book for hot stock tips for 2010, 2011, 2018, or 2035. Any book claiming to provide them is a fairy tale. Rather, this book provides a workable, repeatable framework for increasing the likelihood of finding profitable opportunities in the Consumer Staples sector. And the good news is the investing methodology presented here works for all investing sectors and the broader market. This methodology should serve you not only this year or next, but the whole of your investing career. So good luck and enjoy the journey.

Ken Fisher
CEO of Fisher Investments
Author of the *New York Times* Best Sellers
The Ten Roads to Riches and *The Only Three Questions That Count*

Preface

The *Fisher Investments On* series is designed to provide individual investors, students, and aspiring investment professionals the tools necessary to understand and analyze investment opportunities, primarily for investing in global stocks.

Within the framework of a *top-down* investment method (more on that in Chapter 7), each guide is an easily accessible primer to economic sectors, regions, or other components of the global stock market. While this guide is specifically on Consumer Staples, the basic investment methodology is applicable for analyzing any global sector, regardless of the current macroeconomic environment.

Why a top-down method? Vast evidence shows high-level, or *macro*, investment decisions are ultimately more important portfolio performance drivers than individual stocks. In other words, before picking stocks, investors can benefit greatly by first deciding if stocks are the best investment relative to other assets (like bonds or cash) and then choosing categories of stocks most likely to perform best on a forward-looking basis.

For example, a Technology sector stock picker in 1998 and 1999 probably saw his picks soar as investors cheered the so-called "New Economy." However, from 2000 to 2002, he probably lost his shirt. Was he just smarter in 1998 and 1999? Did his analysis turn bad somehow? Unlikely. What mattered most was stocks in general (and especially US technology stocks) did great in the late 1990s and poorly entering the new century. In other words, a top-down perspective on the broader economy was key to navigating markets—stock picking just wasn't as important.

Fisher Investments on Consumer Staples will help guide you in making top-down investment decisions specifically for the Consumer

Staples sector. It shows how to determine optimal times to invest in Consumer Staples, what industries and sub-industries are likelier to do best, and how individual stocks can benefit in various environments. The global Consumer Staples sector is complex, including a handful of sub-industries and many countries, each with their own unique characteristics. Using our framework, you should be better equipped to critically analyze the sector, spot opportunities, and avoid major pitfalls.

This book takes a global approach to Consumer Staples investing. Most US investors typically invest the majority of their assets in domestic securities; they forget America is less than half of the world market by weight—over 50 percent of investment opportunities are outside our borders. Many of the world's largest Consumer Staples firms are based in foreign nations, including several in emerging markets. For those domiciled on domestic soil, a large percentage of sales is often derived overseas. Simply stated, it is vital to maintain a global perspective when investing in Consumer Staples today.

USING YOUR CONSUMER STAPLES GUIDE

This guide is arranged into three sections. Part 1, "Getting Started in Consumer Staples," discusses fundamental sector basics and Consumer Staples' high-level drivers. Here we'll discuss basic tenets of the Consumer Staples sector, including a detailed explanation about the economic notion of elasticity and an introduction to common strategic attributes enjoyed by successful firms operating in the sector. We will also delve into a historical survey of key transition periods that helped shape the modern Consumer Staples sector. The introductory section of the guide then finishes up with an overview of vital economic, political, and sentiment drivers of the sector.

Part 2, "Next Steps: Consumer Staples Details," builds on the foundational knowledge from Part 1, opening the door to more granular sector analysis. We'll take you through the global Consumer Staples sector investment universe and its diverse components. Firms operating in this sector are similar because they tend to be relatively non-economically cyclical, but diverse in scope, including manufacturers from various levels of the supply chain and retailers. We'll take you through each industry of the sector in detail in explaining how they operate and what specifically drives each industry—so you can analyze the current operating environment and have a rational basis for choosing which industry will most likely outperform or underperform looking forward. Part 2 will also expose you to unique challenges faced by firms operating in the Consumer Staples sector and provide a detailed account of the unique state of consumer products in emerging markets.

Part 3, "Thinking Like a Portfolio Manager," delves into a top-down investment methodology and individual security analysis. You'll learn to ask important questions like: What are the most important elements to consider when analyzing Consumer Staples firms? What are the greatest risks and red flags? This book gives you a step-by-step process to help differentiate firms so you can identify those with the greatest probability of outperforming. We'll also discuss a few investment strategies to help determine when and how to overweight specific sub-industries within the sector.

Note: We've specifically kept the strategies presented here high level so you can return to the book for guidance no matter the market conditions. But we also can't possibly address every market scenario and how markets may change over time. And many additional considerations should be taken into account when crafting a portfolio strategy, including your own investment goals, your time horizon, and other factors unique to you. Therefore, you shouldn't rely solely on the strategies and pointers addressed here because they won't always apply. Rather, this book is intended to provide general guidance and help you to begin thinking critically not only about the Consumer Staples sector, but investing in general.

Further, *Fisher Investments on Consumer Staples* won't give you a silver bullet for always picking the best stocks. The fact is, the right Consumer Staples stocks will be different in different climates and situations. Instead, this guide provides a framework for understanding the sector and its industries so that you can be dynamic and find information the market hasn't yet priced in. There won't be any stock recommendations, target prices, or even a suggestion whether now is a good time to be invested in the sector. The goal is to provide you with tools to make these decisions for yourself, now and in the future. Ultimately, our aim is to give you the framework for repeated, successful investing.

Acknowledgments

No book is ever the product of just one or two people, and we extend our sincere gratitude to a number of colleagues and business associates for their help in making this book a reality.

First, we thank Ken Fisher for providing this wonderful opportunity. There are also a number of Fisher Investments colleagues instrumental to this project, each deserving of praise and thanks. First, a big thank you to Nader Farzan, who helped produce most of the graphs you will find in this book. We also owe special thanks to Michael Hanson and Lara Hoffmans, whose patient mentoring and editing were integral in bringing this book from the idea stage to completion. Dina Ezzat deserves praise for helping manage the on-time delivery of the book, while also offering much appreciated assistance with source citations. Evelyn Chea helped put the finishing touches on the book by offering her editorial expertise. Leila Amiri brought valuable graphic design contributions in coming up with the graphics that appear in the book. Michael Sanberg and Tom Holmes particularly assisted Michael Cannivet in helping carry out his full-time research responsibilities while he was working on the book. Special thanks also go to the team that brought Fisher Investments Press to life—Marc Haberman, Molly Lienesch, and Fabrizio Ornani.

Of course this book would also not be possible without our data vendors, so we owe a debt of gratitude to Thomson Datastream, Thomson Reuters, and Global Financial Data in particular for their permissions. We'd also like to extend our appreciation to our team at Wiley for their support and guidance throughout this project, especially David Pugh and Kelly O'Connor.

Last, Michael would also like to thank his wife Jennifer, who edited the first copies of this book in their earliest form and probably learned more about the Consumer Staples sector than she ever bargained for in the process. This book could not have been completed without her unwavering love and support.

Fisher Investments on Consumer Staples

GETTING STARTED IN CONSUMER STAPLES

CONSUMER STAPLES BASICS

J *oe Consumer has one thing on his mind at 6:10 Monday morning: Coffee. Lulled by the drip of the coffeemaker, Joe idly listens to the news. After his first cup, Joe pours himself some Wheaties—the "Breakfast of Champions." He stares at the bright orange box, recalling childhood dreams of becoming the next athlete to grace the front. Waking from his nostalgia, Joe quickly showers and shaves. He's chagrined to discover he's out of deodorant—his wife's deodorant is the only alternative. (Hopefully, they mean it when they say "strong enough for a man.") Next, he brushes his teeth but is bothered by his reflection—his hair is paying homage to Alfalfa. He gels his cowlick and is out the door 10 minutes behind schedule, as usual.*

Your morning routine may be similar to Joe's. The day-to-day items you use and the investment potential inherent in these products are the focus of this book. Coffee manufacturers, food and toothpaste firms, and a host of other businesses all fit into the global Consumer Staples sector.

This book casts a spotlight on the countless investment ideas found in the myriad products you have in your kitchen, bathroom, and workplace. Of the 10 standard investing sectors, Consumer Staples arguably plays the most active role in daily life. Many of the firms making the products you use daily are publicly traded and can be an integral part of your portfolio.

This chapter will highlight some Consumer Staples basics, including what makes some consumer products *staples* and others *discretionary*—particularly focusing on the concept of *elasticity*. We'll also view long-term sector performance trends and analyze a very famous investor's take on Consumer Staples stocks.

OVERVIEW

Each investing sector has a unique set of attributes. The Industrials sector, for example, is generally capital intensive and economically sensitive. The Energy sector is highly dependent on the supply and demand for oil, while the Technology sector is innovation driven, with a degree of economic cyclicality. So what characterizes the Consumer Staples sector?

Some common characteristics: First, this sector's products have a common end market—consumers. Second, like Joe Consumer, these are products many folks use daily. Finally, frequency of use tends to be consistent for these products, regardless of how the economy is doing.

Note: This isn't to say Consumer Staples is inherently superior to other sectors—it isn't. But Consumer Staples, like each sector, has unique attributes leading both to outperformance and underperformance depending on economic and market conditions. There will be periods when Consumer Staples performs very well relative to the broad market and periods when it lags. The aim of this book is to give you tools to help better predict when that happens and why.

A Big Target Market

Relative to some other standard investing sectors, Consumer Staples has a huge target market. Consumer spending represents about 70 percent of the US's gross domestic product (GDP), as shown in

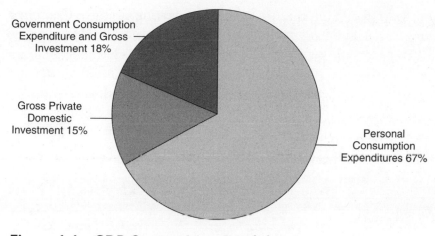

Figure 1.1   GDP Composition Breakdown
Source: US Department of Commerce Bureau of Economic Analysis.

Figure 1.1. It's tough to get a much larger target market than selling directly to consumers.

Not only do Consumer Staples firms have vast potential target markets, but the goods they produce can be ubiquitous. Staples products are nearly everywhere—home, work, stores, restaurants, and so on. Purchasing these items is a natural routine of most grocery store trips and can be an automatic decision based on brand familiarity. Finally, consumption patterns for staples—which are generally viewed as basic necessities—tend to be recession resistant and more stable over time relative to other standard investing sectors.

Sector Composition

Consumer Staples can be broken down into three main categories: Food, Beverage & Tobacco (grouped as one category); Household & Personal Products; and Food & Staples Retailers. (Chapter 4 will cover each of these industries and sub-industries in greater detail.) Table 1.1 lists just a few familiar firms and some of their best-known brands, and the 10 largest global Staples firms (by market cap) are listed in Table 1.2.

Table 1.1   Examples of Companies & Products by Industry

Company	Industry	Product
Kraft	Food	Kraft Macaroni & Cheese
Kellogg	Food	Kellogg's Corn Flakes
Nestlé	Food	Nestlé Toll House Cookies
Coca-Cola	Beverage	Coca-Cola Classic
Pepsi-Cola	Beverage	Diet Pepsi
Anheuser-Busch	Beverage	Budweiser
Philip Morris	Tobacco	Marlboro
RJ Reynolds	Tobacco	Camel
Procter & Gamble	Household Products	Tide laundry detergent
Kimberly-Clark	Household Products	Huggies diapers
L'Oréal	Personal Products	Garnier
Estée Lauder	Personal Products	Clinique
Wal-Mart	Food & Staples Retailers	Diversified staples retailing
Kroger	Food & Staples Retailers	Grocery stores
CVS Caremark	Food & Staples Retailers	Drug retailing

Table 1.2   Top 10 Consumer Staples Firms

Name	Country	Market Value US$ (billions)
Wal-Mart Stores	US	$222.0
Procter & Gamble Co	US	$184.7
Nestlé	Switzerland	$174.2
Coca-Cola Co	US	$120.4
Philip Morris Int'l	US	$105.1
PepsiCo	US	$101.4
British American Tobacco	UK	$67.3
L'Oréal	France	$64.9
CVS Caremark	US	$56.9
Tesco	UK	$56.4

Source: Thomson Datastream; MSCI, Inc.[1] as of 06/30/2008.

STAPLES' DISTANT COUSIN—CONSUMER DISCRETIONARY

Consumer Staples and Consumer Discretionary are a little like cousins—part of the same general family (consumer oriented), but not much in common beyond that.

Consumer Discretionary firms include automobile manufacturers like General Motors, apparel stores like Gap, national restaurant chains like the Cheesecake Factory, and large entertainment firms like Disney. The primary difference between the two sectors is Staples firms produce goods deemed as necessities (soap, cereal, bottled water), while Discretionary firms produce goods deemed as non-necessities (cars, clothing, laptops). This difference can be examined more critically by comparing them in terms of *elasticity*.

Elasticity

Elasticity is a measure of one variable's sensitivity to a change in another variable. The term references changes in demand relative to changes in price or income. The concept of elasticity is core to understanding what makes the Consumer Staples sector tick.

Elasticity can be calculated two basic ways:

$$\text{Income Elastcity} = \frac{\%\,\text{change in quantity}}{\%\,\text{change in income}}$$

$$\text{Price Elastcity} = \frac{\%\,\text{change in quantity}}{\%\,\text{change in price}}$$

If elasticity is greater than or equal to 1 in either calculation, then the demand curve is considered *elastic*. If it is less than 1, it's *inelastic*.

Consumer Staples products are *inelastic*—necessities purchased by consumers regardless of how their personal economic situation shifts over time. Discretionary products are just the opposite—*elastic*—since income or price fluctuations do materially impact consumer demand.

Income Elasticity   How can income and price elasticity drive buying decisions? Back to our friend, Joe Consumer. Joe just got a promotion and a 20 percent increase to his current salary of $70,000 a year. Joe is excited—instead of just one annual family vacation, he figures they can now afford two per year. Here's how the elasticity of Joe's travel mathematically works out, using the income elasticity equation:

$$\text{Income elasticity} = \frac{(2-1)/1}{(84,000-70,000)/70,000}$$
$$= 100\%/20\%$$
$$= 5$$

With an elasticity of 5, Joe's travel is highly elastic—like most of the broad population. This means that during strong economic times, when many people see wage increases, travel in general shoots up, positively influencing hotels, rental car firms, and so on. Note these are all Consumer Discretionary industries.

Now let's look at how this raise impacts another aspect of Joe's life—his soda consumption. Joe usually drinks a six-pack of Coke per week. He doesn't suddenly start drinking twice the number of Cokes just because he got a raise. A six-pack per week is still fine. Here's how the income elasticity calculation works in this instance:

$$\text{Income elasticity} = \frac{(6-6)/6}{(84,000-70,000)/70,000}$$
$$= 0\%/20\%$$
$$= 0$$

With an elasticity calculation of zero in this example, Coke (a Consumer Staples product) has an inelastic demand relationship to Joe's income.

Note that most investors are unlikely to run elasticity calculations like this in their day-to-day analysis. Nevertheless, the example serves as a practical demonstration of what makes some goods more elastic than others.

Price Elasticity   Price elasticity plays a similar role to income elasticity. A price increase will act as a demand deterrent to consumers of discretionary products because as the price of the product escalates, so does the opportunity cost of buying the product. (*Opportunity cost* is what you give up to get what you want, whether it's time, money, etc.)

An example of price elasticity in relation to a discretionary product: What happens to Joe's vacation plans if energy costs spike? One obvious result—he must pay more for his family's airfares. Consequently, he may postpone his family trip until prices drop a bit or he might take a cheaper vacation than originally planned.

How does price elasticity figure in relation to one of Joe's favorite Consumer Staples items—Coca-Cola? Increased energy costs affect this too. Since Coke now has to pay more to distribute its products, it will likely raise its prices, just like the airlines. Dollar-wise, however, this price increase has a much smaller impact on Joe's overall budget, so he'll probably keep drinking the same number of Cokes every week.

Elasticity From an Investment Standpoint   These examples underscore why Consumer Staples stocks can perform better relatively during tumultuous economic periods: When the economy contracts, wages can come under pressure, diminishing demand for many goods. Inflation is another phenomenon that can impact prices—if prices rise faster than wages can keep pace, demand can decrease.

Both of these have the power to materially diminish demand for products across most sectors (not just Consumer Discretionary). But historically, demand holds up relatively well in the Consumer Staples sector. For this reason, investors often seek "safe haven" here. While sales or earnings might not expand much in an economic downturn, the relative price to earnings (P/E) multiple of the sector often rises as investors begin to place more of a premium on earnings consistency. (We will cover this phenomenon in greater detail later.)

Price Elasticity of Demand

The price elasticity of demand is influenced by three primary determinants.

1. Price relative to income. If the price of an item is high in proportion to one's income, then price changes will be important.

   Example: Airline travel and new cars are expensive, so even a small percentage change in their prices can have a big impact on a consumer's budget and consumption patterns. Shampoo, however, is a small percentage of the average consumer's income; hence, it tends to be price inelastic.

2. Availability of substitutes. The greater the number of substitute products, the more elastic goods tend to be.

   Example: Fish is fairly elastic since consumers can always eat more beef, chicken, or pork if fish prices rise sharply. Cigarettes, however, are fairly inelastic, since most smokers can't imagine any other product that could easily substitute for a cigarette.

3. Time. When consumers have more time to adjust their consumption patterns, price elasticity tends to increase.

   Example: The quantity of gasoline demanded doesn't immediately fall much when gasoline prices rise, since consumers cannot easily trade in their current vehicle for a more fuel efficient one. However, if gas prices stay high for a number of years, this tendency slowly begins to change, because with more time, consumers are better able to adjust their consumption habits. Therefore, the long-run price elasticity of demand is higher than short-run elasticity.

THE BUSINESS CYCLE'S WINDS OF CHANGE

We've discussed the different levels of economic sensitivity when comparing the Consumer Staples sector to Consumer Discretionary and how this can favor Staples firms in a slower economy. Now let's touch on how economic seasonality can work against the Staples sector.

In a robust economy, Staples firms are at a disadvantage relative to other sectors because they find top-line sales growth harder to come by. Further, profit margins in several of the Staples industries can be thinner compared to Discretionary firms. Based on these differences, Consumer Discretionary stocks can bring more portfolio upside if the economy is expected to be rosy, since sales and profits can ramp up in a hurry for many of these firms. Staples firms, on the other hand, tend to maintain their steady pace. During strengthening economic periods, investors typically shift away from the Consumer Staples sector and place a higher premium on sectors leveraged to economic upside.

P/E versus P/E

The average P/E ratio of the Consumer Staples sector over the last 10 years (1998–2007) is 22.4, whereas Discretionary traded at 26.0 times trailing earnings.

Table 1.3 shows that out of the 10 years there were three years where Consumer Staples traded at a higher multiple than Consumer Discretionary: 1998, 2000, and 2007. 1998 saw a massive stock market correction and both 2000 and 2007 marked the beginning of bear markets.

Table 1.3   Consumer Discretionary vs. Consumer Staples P/E Comparison

Year	Consumer Discretionary P/E	Consumer Staples P/E
1998	27.6	28.1
1999	33.5	25.5
2000	25.6	28.0
2001	36.9	24.3
2002	31.1	17.3
2003	25.4	20.4
2004	20.4	20.1
2005	20.2	19.6
2006	21.9	19.9
2007	18.0	20.3
Average	26.0	22.4

Source: Thomson Datastream; MSCI, Inc.[2]

Wal-Mart's Fashion Foray

"If at first you don't succeed, try, try again"—a good summary of Wal-Mart's continual attempts to penetrate the higher-value apparel market. In 2006, Wal-Mart placed expensive ads in *Vogue* and debuted new apparel offerings at New York's Fashion Week. However, the company soon discovered that core Wal-Mart shoppers were no fashionistas and were unwilling to pay big bucks for designer clothing. Sales were weak and overstocked inventories became a drag on earnings.

Despite this setback, Wal-Mart was at it again two years later—trying to intertwine more expensive clothing into its discount-oriented stores. The new message emphasizes both fashion and quality at an affordable price. Why the persistence?

Apparel remains attractive to Wal-Mart because as the company builds fewer stores, it must generate more profits from existing stores. Discretionary products like high-end clothing have higher profit margins than traditional Wal-Mart merchandise, which includes an assortment of Staples items. The clothing line profit margins are estimated to be about 31 percent—a full 10 percentage points ahead of all the other categories the discounter sells.

Source: Ann Zimmerman and Cheryl Lu-Lien Tan, "After Misstep, Wal-Mart Revisits Fashion," *Wall Street Journal* (April 24, 2008).

Staples Stock Performance Versus Discretionary

Given what we now know about how different the Consumer Staples and Consumer Discretionary sectors are, how do you think their stock performances stack up? Figure 1.2 provides a snapshot over the last 10 years, using the MSCI World Index as a proxy.

There are a couple noteworthy periods:

1. From mid-1998 to the end of 1999, Discretionary trounced Staples in relative performance.
2. As the bear market ensued in 2000, Discretionary sold off precipitously while Staples gained ground.
3. Discretionary bounced more sharply when the next bull market came to life, rising at a faster pace than Staples through 2003.

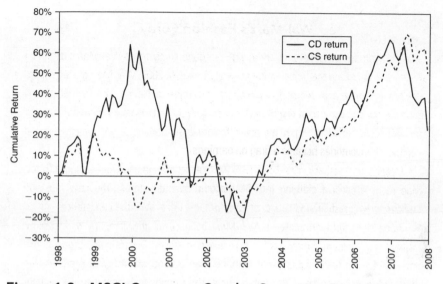

Figure 1.2   MSCI Consumer Staples Sector vs. Discretionary Over the Last 10 Years
Source: Thomson Datastream; MSCI, Inc.[3]

4. Staples and Discretionary both rallied as the bull market progressed over the next couple years, with Discretionary maintaining a slight lead.

The next big divergence happened in late 2007, when the recent bear market started. Discretionary fell much more sharply than Staples through the first two quarters of 2008 (Figure 1.2 stops at 7/1/2008).

Now let's break open the anatomy behind what can drive share price performance differentials by looking at price movement, earnings-per-share (EPS) growth, and relative P/E multiple expansion and contraction between the two sectors. For the purposes of this exercise, we'll look at the period of 6/30/2007 to 6/30/2008.

Table 1.4 shows MSCI World Consumer Discretionary and Consumer Staples cumulative monthly returns as the bear market began to take shape in late 2007.

Discretionary stocks sold off close to 10 percent by the end of 2007. Meanwhile, Staples rallied. By the time the first half of 2008

Table 1.4 MSCI World Consumer Discretionary vs. Consumer Staples (6/30/2007–6/30/2008)

Date	MSCI World Consumer Discretionary Index	MSCI World Consumer Staples Index	CD Cumulative Percentage Return	CS Cumulative Percentage Return
6/30/2007	132.686	128.383		
7/31/2007	128.141	125.927	–3.4%	–1.9%
8/31/2007	126.262	129.015	–4.8%	0.5%
9/28/2007	128.624	134.207	–3.1%	4.5%
10/31/2007	132.030	138.376	–0.5%	7.8%
11/30/2007	124.045	140.801	–6.5%	9.7%
12/31/2007	119.753	139.380	–9.7%	8.6%
1/31/2008	112.147	129.853	–15.5%	1.1%
2/29/2008	110.214	130.907	–16.9%	2.0%
3/31/2008	108.577	134.231	–18.2%	4.6%
4/30/2008	110.885	134.137	–16.4%	4.5%
5/30/2008	111.526	134.743	–15.9%	5.0%
6/30/2008	98.926	123.956	**–25.4%**	**–3.4%**

Source: Thomson Datastream; MSCI, Inc.[4]

concluded, Discretionary had fallen 25.4 percent, compared to a modest Staples decline of 3.4 percent.

What drove this vast performance differential? During times of distress and particularly during bear markets, investors place a premium on the earnings consistency of Consumer Staples stocks. Between 6/30/2007 and 6/30/2008, as the world economy began slowing, both sectors were able to continue growing their earnings (although Consumer Staples grew at a stronger pace). The MSCI World Consumer Staples constituent universe grew its EPS by 15.1 percent, while the MSCI World Consumer Discretionary universe grew its EPS by 12.0 percent.

Along the way, valuations began changing. Investors became willing to pay less for both sectors' earnings as their outlook deteriorated and risk aversion heightened. During the 12-month period,

Table 1.5   Anatomy of Price Performance—CS vs. CD (6/30/2007–6/30/2008)

	Price Performance	EPS Growth	P/E Multiple
Consumer Staples	–3.5%	+15.1%	–17%
Consumer Discretionary	–25.4%	+12.0%	–39%

Source: Thomson Datastream; MSCI, Inc.[5]

the P/E ratio for Staples fell from 20.0 on 6/30/2007 to 16.6 on 6/30/2008 (a 17 percent decline). Consumer Discretionary, however, saw far more severe multiple contraction while investors were fleeing for safety, with the sector's P/E falling from 22.6 to 13.8 (a 39 percent decline).

It's important to remember that earnings and valuation are both determinants of price performance. Table 1.5 breaks down the anatomy of the two sectors' price performances over the period.

BORING CAN BE BEAUTIFUL

Can you think of any new soap product that has come along lately and lit the world on fire? Probably not. But you can probably name a few trendy cars that have recently come to market. You might be thinking: "These Staples companies sound boring. I'd rather have high-growth companies in my portfolio. Isn't that what investing is all about—finding the next hot growth area?" Not necessarily.

Due to their defensive nature, most Staples stocks are unlikely to become short-term portfolio home runs. But that doesn't mean Staples don't play an important role in a top-down portfolio strategy. Over time, all investing categories should yield similar returns—they just travel different paths to get there.

The Original S&P 500

One feature of Staples firms is, if successful, they can prosper for a long time. In his 2005 book, *The Future for Investors*, Jeremy Siegel analyzed the long-term performance of the original S&P 500 stocks from 1957. He noted that, because of the power of compounding returns, if you'd put $1,000 in an S&P 500 Index fund (had such a thing existed) on February 28, 1957, and left it alone until December 31, 2003, your $1,000 would have become almost $125,000 in today's dollars. Not a bad investment!

But what if you were lucky enough to put your $1,000 into the top-performing stock of the original S&P 500? You'd end up with almost $4.6 million! That firm was cigarette-maker Philip Morris.[6] Often derided as one of the foremost "sin stocks," this Consumer Staples giant has endured and rewarded investors handsomely through the years.

Table 1.6 illustrates the 20 best-performing, surviving firms of the original S&P 500 through 2003, showing annual return averages and the value of an original investment of $1,000 made on February 28, 1957.[7]

Staples firms claim 11 out of top 20 spots. These long-term survivors share several traits, including:

- Strong brands based on widespread name recognition and consumer trust. Brand power is highly beneficial because it deflects substitution effects and fosters above-average returns on capital.
- Durable, lasting businesses that generated recurring revenue growth in good times and bad.
- Successful international expansion.
- These firms are strong generators of free cash flow. Finance theory suggests value for an asset is the present value of all future cash flows. Higher cash flow should correspond with higher value.

Realize this study is not justification to load up only on Consumer Staples stocks for the long haul. There are optimal times to own more or less of the sector, and the odds of successfully picking only standouts and holding them year after year are slim.

Table 1.6   Top 20 Performing S&P 500 Survivors, 1957–2003

Rank	2003 Name	Sector	Accumulation of $1,000	Annual Return
1	**Philip Morris**	**Consumer Staples**	$4,626,402	19.75%
2	Abbott Labs	Health Care	$1,281,335	16.51%
3	Bristol-Myers Squibb	Health Care	$1,209,445	16.36%
4	**Tootsie Roll Industries**	**Consumer Staples**	$1,090,955	16.11%
5	Pfizer	Health Care	$1,054,823	16.03%
6	**Coca-Cola**	**Consumer Staples**	$1,051,646	16.02%
7	Merck	Health Care	$1,003,410	15.90%
8	**PepsiCo**	**Consumer Staples**	$866,068	15.54%
9	**Colgate-Palmolive**	**Consumer Staples**	$761,163	15.22%
10	Crane	Industrials	$736,796	15.14%
11	**HJ Heinz**	**Consumer Staples**	$635,988	14.78%
12	**Wrigley**	**Consumer Staples**	$603,877	14.65%
13	Fortune Brands	Consumer Discretionary	$580,025	14.55%
14	**Kroger**	**Consumer Staples**	$546,793	14.41%
15	Schering-Plough	Health Care	$537,050	14.36%
16	**Procter & Gamble**	**Consumer Staples**	$513,752	14.26%
17	**Hershey Foods**	**Consumer Staples**	$507,001	14.22%
18	Wyeth	Health Care	$461,186	13.99%
19	Royal Dutch Petroleum	Energy	$398,837	13.64%
20	**General Mills**	**Consumer Staples**	$388,425	13.58%
	S&P 500		$124,486	10.85%

Source: Jeremy Siegel, *The Future for Investors* (Random House Publishing: 2005).

On a Roll

If you'd invested in Tootsie Roll Industries (Ticker: TR) from 1957 to 2003, you'd have handily beat the stock market. Tootsie Roll returned an annualized 16.1 percent, while the S&P 500 returned an annualized 10.9 percent. Not bad for a sticky little candy.

Austrian immigrant Leo Hirshfield created the original Tootsie Roll in 1896 and named it after his daughter, Tootsie. Today, the company produces a daily average of 62 million Tootsie Rolls and more than 16 million lollipops.

Source: Hoover's.

Economic Moats   Long ago, moats of water served as protective barriers by shielding castles from invaders. More recently, Warren Buffett popularized the term "economic moat," an analogy referring to a business's ability to maintain competitive advantages versus its peers, thereby protecting long-term profits and market share. A competitive advantage can take many forms. The important thing to remember is it allows a firm to provide a good or service similar to its competitors while simultaneously outperforming those competitors in profit generation.

Buffett, whose investment portfolio at Berkshire Hathaway is concentrated in consumer franchises, describes the concept of an economic moat in his 2007 Annual Shareholder Letter (page 6), writing:

> A truly great business must have an enduring "moat" that protects excellent returns on invested capital. The dynamics of capitalism guarantee that competitors will repeatedly assault any business "castle" that is earning high returns. Therefore a formidable barrier such as a company's being the low-cost producer (GEICO, Costco) or possessing a world-wide brand (Coca-Cola, Gillette, American Express) is essential for sustained success.

Berkshire's portfolio is also purposefully weighted to firms operating in "steady" industries, like Consumer Staples. Berkshire's criterion of "enduring" causes them to avoid firms operating in industries prone to rapid and continual change, where economic moats might not be as sustainable. An example of a steady firm with a competitive advantage is See's Candies, detailed in the nearby box.

In the final three chapters of this book, we'll dissect a variety of strategic attributes to look for when researching Consumer Staples. The stronger the arsenal of competitive advantages a firm has, the wider its economic moat.

Oh, Say Can You See's?

Under Buffett's ownership, See's Candies has done a good job of consistently expanding profitability. In 1972, See's Candies made about 25 cents of pre-tax earnings per pound of chocolate sold. By 1998, the profit per pound had increased to $2, representing an annual growth rate of roughly 8.3 percent. In addition, See's volume grew over the same period from about 16 million pounds sold per year to 30 million. That's an annual growth rate of about 2.4 percent. Add them together and you have a company generating 11 percent average annual earnings growth.

What's the secret to See's enduring success? Buffett bought See's because he saw the company had a strong economic moat based on ultra-loyal customers. Buffett coveted See's customer goodwill because it meant the company had considerable pricing power, which could drive attractive long-term earnings growth with virtually no major capital requirements necessary to finance the growth. (Note: Most businesses have working capital requirements that increase in proportion to sales growth; See's is an exception.)

Upon assuming ownership, Buffett capitalized on See's economic moat and confidently increased prices every year on December 26th. Volume continued to grow modestly over time, but pricing was the key contributor to profit growth (as is the case with many Staples products). After all, when husbands are in the doghouse and have to buy their wives their favorite candy, they likely won't quibble over small incremental price changes, even if they do add up through the years.

Individual investors trying to imitate Buffett's success with See's might have a hard time—unless they have enough cash on hand to wholly buy a firm. As a subsidiary of Berkshire Hathaway, See's isn't publicly traded.

Source: Emil Lee, "How Buffett Made a Killing in Chocolate," *The Motley Fool* (November 15, 2007).

Chapter Recap

You've now been introduced to some of the fundamental characteristics distinguishing the Consumer Staples sector. We will build upon many of the concepts presented in this chapter as we progress into later chapters. The Consumer Staples sector is made up of industries serving everyday consumers.

(Continued)

- Most products produced in this sector are ingrained in our culture as basic necessities.

- The Consumer Staples sector is comprised of various industries, including Food, Beverage & Tobacco, Household & Personal Products, and Food & Staples Retailers.

- Demand in the sector is characterized as price and income inelastic, which makes the sector non-economically sensitive and differentiates Consumer Staples products from Consumer Discretionary products.

- Consumer Staples stocks usually will not provide tremendous upside over a short time horizon, but firms with strong economic moats can be lucrative long-term investments.

HISTORY OF CONSUMERISM IN AMERICA

"As soon as you can familiarize yourself with the actions of the past, you will be able to anticipate and act correctly and profitably upon forthcoming movements."
—Legendary Wall Street speculator, Jesse Livermore

To understand where you may be going, you need to understand where you've been. That's Jesse Livermore's basic message. In his quest to anticipate the anticipation of others, Livermore, a renowned stock speculator from the early twentieth century, carefully studied historical stock performance while keeping an eye toward the future. Whether studying historical market cycles or merely brushing up on basic sector history, the past can help you better understand the present and future.

This chapter will trace the evolution of the consumer goods industry starting from the American Revolution. Along the way, we'll cover the transformative underpinnings that created the present consumer goods universe. Though the Consumer Staples sector may seem slow to change compared to sector peers, it in fact evolves continuously. The firms and investors who anticipate future consumer shifts can be the ones best positioned to capitalize on change from an investment standpoint.

COLONIAL AMERICA AND CONSUMERISM

Think the age of consumerism is something new? No way! Consumerism is as old as the colonies.

The lifestyle differences between people who lived during the Middle Ages and those who lived in Colonial America are almost unimaginable. Both were tough environments by today's standards, lacking most modern amenities and comforts. If you could use a time machine to transport yourself back, it probably wouldn't take long for you to transport yourself back to today.

Standard of living did improve a lot during the Colonial Era, however. Before the American Revolution in the late seventeenth and early eighteenth centuries, myriad factors combined to make new consumer goods available to the mass population—some call this period the "Consumer Revolution." With rising incomes in the colonies came rising expectations. As society became nimbler, social rank was determined by more than just houses, land, and livestock. The colonialists had access to personal care products and foods never dreamed of before.

In many ways, this period gave birth to the Consumer Staples industry we recognize today as new standards related to consumer necessities emerged in response to an improving economy.

Economic Drivers

When England established the colony of Virginia to capitalize on its vast natural resources and agricultural potential, Jamestown became a hotbed of commercial activity, particularly for tobacco. Tobacco became one of America's first major exports. Surging tobacco sales overseas also enabled more trade possibilities when it came to importing foreign goods as Virginians bought more manufactured goods from England.

The Tobacco Inspection Act was passed in 1730, with the goal of centralizing tobacco exports at inspection warehouses for quality control. An unexpected side effect of the Act was early development of retail businesses throughout the colony. Merchants quickly established networks of stores where tobacco could be purchased and imported goods could be sold year round to nearby customers. Another byproduct of this centralization was the early establishment of credit facilities. Small planters no longer had to wait to sell their tobacco when the annual fleet arrived—they used tobacco notes from warehouses to establish credit, allowing them to purchase goods whenever they desired. By the middle of the eighteenth century, complex distribution and credit systems took shape across Virginia. Imports continued surging. In fact, six years after the warehouses were established, imports had nearly doubled.[1]

Materialism Spreads in America

With economic changes came social changes. The New World was a free and mostly unfettered frontier, operating independently from the mercantilism-dominated centers of the world. Colonial America broke from the societal boundaries of its European heritage, shedding previous cultural hierarchies based on family lineages.

This shift emboldened a new spirit of materialism that quickly spread throughout the colonies. Common citizens felt like they had the power to distinguish themselves by owning an array of fashionable consumer goods. A constant wave of immigrants permeated the colonies, reinforcing demand for relatively inexpensive, fashionable goods that could be used frequently as demonstrations of status.

Use of many personal care items like cosmetics and perfume became more common as both began to be manufactured in America.

Previously, women made their own makeup based on their own formulas. Some we might find a bit strange today: Poor frontier women used bacon grease to manage their complexions, beet juice to color their lips, and flour to lighten their skin.

People weren't very hygienic in Colonial America by today's standards, but they did realize the benefits of soap and often made their own out of wood ashes and animal fat. They also did laundry. Women would scrub clothing by hand, find a place for the clothes to dry, then use hand irons heated with coals and held with padding to press the clothing. Laundry starch was a chore to make, usually derived from drawing starch from potatoes in a multi-day process—not terrifically convenient. Later on, sugar became a substitute for starching, but in colonial times, sugar was a scarce commodity.[2]

Some beverages, like tea, apple cider, and beer, became more popular and ingrained in American culture in the eighteenth century. Most homes had a water barrel that the entire family drank from and also used to brush their teeth. Teeth brushing usually involved using a piece of cloth and some salt and baking soda, if available.

Food staple items also began emerging in Colonial America. In the confectionary realm, sugar candy, sugar-coated nuts, and toffee were all enjoyed. Other popular sweets that saw widespread adoption around this time included preserves, jams, jellies, small cakes, cookies, and ice cream.[3] Typical breakfast and dinner meals differed by household (there was no such thing as "lunch" in the Colonial Era), but they often included an assortment of meats, stews, and vegetables. While the food types varied during this era, food customs were becoming more homogenous than they had been previously. In fact, America's first cookbook was published around this time. Food historians generally agree that Amelia Simmons' *American Cookery* (Hartford, 1796) represents the first "American" cookbook—it was the first to include indigenous ingredients.[4]

The popularity and growing use of a range of new products (which were becoming "staples of society") were based largely on a higher spirit of self-entitlement and new views of what it meant to be "ladies and gentlemen of society." Thomas Jefferson went so far as to call eighteenth century Williamsburg "the finest school of manners and morals that ever existed in America."[5]

It's worth pointing out most Consumer Staples products are only considered "staples" because they have become ingrained into our culture at some point in time. As covered in Chapter 6, things we consider items of standard use were not always so and still aren't in other parts of the world.

Early Advertising

Advertising began to evolve during this period as well. Eighteenth-century ads were quite primitive by today's standards—usually nothing more than a simple announcement of goods on hand. As time progressed, persuasive appeals began to accompany dry product descriptions. Marketers learned to better use ads to lure potential consumers, turning to the only mass communication device of the time—print publications. Newspapers received large-scale distribution and were the best way to market products to a wide audience during the late 1700s and early 1800s.[6]

Ben Franklin—Ad Man

Founding Father Benjamin Franklin invented the lightning rod, bifocals, and . . . modern advertising?

One of the most advanced publications of the Colonial Era was Ben Franklin's *Pennsylvania Gazette*, which tested new formats like placing headlines, illustrations, and advertising alongside editorials. This was a departure from most publications that almost never printed ads wider than a single column and generally eschewed illustrations or even unique typefaces. Consumer goods, given their mass appeal, utilized much of the ad space in papers like Franklin's. Today, he's even considered by some as the "Patron Saint of Advertising."

Source: "Master Marketer," PBS.org.

MASS PRODUCTION IN THE LATE NINETEENTH CENTURY

One of the largest transformations in the consumer products industry happened in the 1800s, when mass production technology emerged during the Industrial Revolution, which gave us mass production and a declining cost curve. By manufacturing a large number of identical items, a firm could spread the fixed cost of their factory operations over many units and also employ low-cost labor. Thus, it became economically feasible, perhaps even imperative, to leverage *economies of scale*—manufacturing large quantities of a good at increasingly lower costs and of consistent quality.

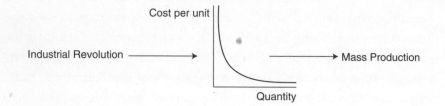

Economies of Scale

The factory system that facilitated economies of scale was a radical departure from the past. Previously, virtually all work was completed by hand in much the same way it had been done for centuries, if not millennia. Then came inventions like the "spinning jenny," a device allowing one person to spin many threads simultaneously, increasing the amount of finished cotton a single worker could produce. Another innovation was James Watts' modern steam engine, which created a new source of power used to run factories.

As production processes became increasingly automated, creative destruction quickly spread. For example, individual hand weavers were driven out of business and replaced by more efficient factories. As factories grew, factory workers became ever more specialized in their functions, leading to the formation of "assembly-line" production. These events gave rise to explosive productivity growth and promulgated scalable advantages across an array of business types, including consumer products manufacturing.

Economies of scale were a vital underpinning behind many of today's dominant Consumer Staples companies that trace their roots to the nineteenth century, including HJ Heinz and Procter & Gamble. Both firms saw their early success magnified as they implemented mass production techniques. As P&G and Heinz began scaling their operations, they were able to produce higher quality goods at lower costs than their competitors. Their swelling size began to provide distribution advantages as well. These advantages further perpetuated their growth and expansion efforts and helped catapult them into leadership positions in their respective industries.

A firm that establishes economies of scale exceeding its peers is like a bicyclist riding downhill. Once the cyclist has started down the hill, momentum builds and he goes faster and faster. The same can be said for a company that establishes scale advantages over its peers. Its scale advantages can lead to faster growth than smaller competitors, which can make it even bigger on a relative basis and propel ever-increasing economies of scale for as long as it continues to execute successfully. This compounding effect is the magic potion that might transform small, family-run businesses into $200 billion global enterprises over time.

There are five input cost advantages created by economies of scale.

1. **Lower input costs.** When a company buys inputs in bulk, it can take advantage of volume discounts not available to smaller competitors.
2. **Costly inputs.** If a company is able to spread costly inputs like research and development and advertising over an increase in its production units (outputs), economies of scale can be realized.
3. **Specialized inputs.** As a company's scale of production increases, the company can employ specialized labor and machinery, resulting in greater efficiency.
4. **Techniques and organizational inputs.** With a larger scale of production, a company may also apply better organizational

skills to its resources, such as a clear-cut chain of command, while improving its production and distribution methods.

5. **Learning inputs.** Similar to improved organization and technique—with time, the learning processes related to production, selling, and distribution can result in improved efficiency.

Advertising in the Late Nineteenth & Early Twentieth Centuries

In the 1880s, industries ranging from soap to canned foods to cigarettes introduced new production techniques, creating standardized products that could be rolled out in unheard-of quantities. Following the advent of mass production techniques, total advertising volume in the US grew from about $200 million in 1880 to nearly $3 billion in 1920 as firms sought new ways to reach larger segments of consumers.[7] Advertising agencies grew in prominence and became trusted advisers as the largest companies sought to increase their national brand recognition.[8]

THE ROARING TWENTIES AND THE CONSUMER ECONOMY (1921–1929)

In the 1920s, the manufacturing and advertising innovations of the previous 40 years began to coalesce, accelerating the transition of America to a mass consumer society. Lifestyles changed rapidly, financial excesses were enjoyed, and technology accelerated at a brisk pace—it was the "Roaring Twenties" indeed.

During the decade, newfound ability to produce goods on a mass scale was met by widespread advancements in transportation. Automobiles proliferated, airplanes emerged, and continued progress was made in rail and ship transportation. These changes improved distribution capabilities for large firms and made consumers more mobile.

Rising Standard of Living

Working people at many income levels experienced a rise in their standard of living. From just 1922 to 1928, the index of industrial production increased 70 percent, while the real wages of employed workers increased a startling 22 percent.[9]

Automobiles, radios, and durable consumer goods like vacuum cleaners and washing machines emerged as some of the top-selling new products of the 1920s, reshaping daily lives. While these products are Consumer Discretionary items, they played a role in shaping the Consumer Staples landscape by opening the door to more prolific use of Staples items.

Electricity infrastructure was installed around the country, helping reduce manufacturing costs and enabling many new goods to come to market. Similar to the Colonial Era, the 1920s saw a higher level of consumer credit available as businesses learned their potential markets were far larger if they were willing to loan a portion of the purchase price to the consumer. Thus, installment credit came into form, increasing purchasing power and propelling widespread adoption of new goods.[10]

Because of the profound impact access to these goods had on this and later periods, it's worthwhile to take a closer look at how autos, radios, and consumer appliances changed the landscape, as well as specific case studies of notable players in each area.

Autos   Retailing was once a very personalized business. Owners of early so-called "mom-and-pop" stores often lived in the same neighborhood as their customers. It was common for shop owners to know their customer's names, where they worked, and their family history. As consumers' mobility increased, so did their choices beyond just the local neighborhood. The days of local mom-and-pop dominance were on their way out.

As roads multiplied and highways began to surface in later years, people migrated from the cities to the suburbs in large numbers. Merchants followed their increasingly mobile customers, rapidly building new shopping centers and forming chains. In 1922, JC Nichols created Country Club Plaza, an automobile-centered plaza built on the outskirts of Kansas City, Missouri. The project was unique because it was built according to a unified plan owned and oper-

America's Love Affair with Cars

Low-cost production techniques and technological superiority led to faster adoption of automobiles in the US when compared to the rest of the world. By 1925, there was one automobile for every six people in the US; and by 1930, the ratio increased to 1 for every 4.6 people. Table 2.1 offers a comparative illustration of the development of motor vehicle production in North America and Europe.

Table 2.1   Motor Vehicle Production

Year	US	Canada	France	UK	Germany	Italy
1907	45,000	3,000	25,000	12,000	4,000	0
1913	485,000	15,000	45,000	34,000	14,000	2,000
1924	3,504,000	135,000	145,000	133,000	18,000	35,000
1928	4,359,000	242,000	210,000	212,000	90,000	55,000
1935	3,971,000	173,000	165,000	404,000	240,000	44,000

Source: J. Bradford DeLong, "Slouching Towards Utopia?: The Economic History of the Twentieth Century," (February 1997).

ated by a single entity rather than a random group of stores. Nichols was the first to popularize the term "shopping center" when describing such commercial sites built for the automobile.[11] Supermarkets like Kroger and drugstores like Walgreens took advantage of the shift, quickly expanding and emerging as leading retailers of food, drugs, and everyday consumer products. Later in the century, Consumer Staples giant Wal-Mart would also emerge as a one-stop-shop consumer destination.

Radios   While automobiles brought mobility to both urban and rural consumers, radios provided access to information and greater connectivity between rural and urban areas. Most important to consumer goods firms, the radio enabled businesses to advertise their products and services to a mass audience, unlocking immense branding opportunities. The following is an excerpt from a study conducted

Titans That Grew Up in the Twentieth Century: Walgreen Co.

In 1901, Chicago pharmacist Charles Walgreen borrowed $2,000 for a down payment on his first drugstore. In 1909, he sold equity in his store so he could buy his second. To differentiate the new store, he installed a soda fountain and began serving lunch. By 1916, he had expanded to seven stores and consolidated under the corporate name Walgreen Co. Walgreen Co. became listed on the NYSE in 1927, and by 1929, 397 stores were open in 87 cities.

The 1950s brought myriad changes to how drugstores did business, and Walgreens was an early leader in self-service merchandising—shoppers located what they wanted without a clerk's assistance.

Today, Walgreen Co. operates over 6,200 stores in 49 states and Puerto Rico and is the top drug retailer in the country by sales. Prescription drugs account for about two-thirds of sales, with the rest from general merchandise, cosmetics, and groceries. Walgreens' strategy is to selectively pick prime locations to build, rather than buy, its stores. As an added shopping convenience, over 80 percent of its stores offer drive-through pharmacies. Walgreens stores are free-standing, making them more visible than those in strip malls, and offer customers ample parking.

The company projects having more than 7,000 stores by 2010 and sees long-term potential for more than 13,000 stores in the US.

Source: Hoover's, Inc.

by advertising firm Erwin, Wasey & Company in the late 1920s that describes the dramatic interconnectivity that emerged as national broadcasting channels grew.

> By far the greatest single development in radio advertising has been the development of network or chain broadcasting. Starting with a single radio station about two years ago the Radio Corporation of America with its allied companies, the Westinghouse Electric and the General Electric have built up a chain of stations that enables an advertiser to reach every section of the country. This company, known as the National Broadcasting Company, through its three main chains and

supplementary cities now has broadcast facilities available in 43 cities.

Another company, known as the Columbia Broadcasting System, offers a chain of 16 stations paralleling in its coverage part of the stations of the National Broadcasting Company. . . . These two large chains carry the great majority of national radio advertising and probably will continue to do so.[12]

The two firms being described are modern media giants, NBC and CBS. Their widespread distribution across major cities was a perfect avenue for firms looking to establish large-scale chains and build brands.

Not surprisingly, Consumer Staples firms were some of the first to heavily embrace radio advertising as they launched their brands nationally. Coca-Cola Co. and Wm. Wrigley Jr. Co. are two examples of early movers in radio advertising, spending $30,098 and $28,000, respectively, on radio ads in 1927.[13]

Titans That Grew Up in the Twentieth Century: The Coca-Cola Company

Coke's original formula was invented in 1886 by Atlanta pharmacist John Pemberton. His bookkeeper named the product after two ingredients: coca leaves and kola nuts. By 1891, druggist Asa Candler purchased the Coca-Cola Company, and within four short years, the soda fountain drink circulated in every US state.

In 1899, Candler sold most US bottling rights for $1 to two gentlemen from Tennessee. The two men designed a regional franchise bottling system that expanded to more than 1,000 bottlers within 20 years. In 1916, Candler retired from the business to serve as mayor of Atlanta and, in 1919, sold Coca-Cola to banker Ernest Woodruff for $25 million—it went public that year.

Coke became such an integral part of American culture that during World War II, the government built 64 overseas bottling plants so soldiers could afford Cokes at a nickel apiece.

Coke's growth rate went into overdrive around 1981, when Roberto Goizueta became chairman. After several shrewd purchases, sales, and new product launches (e.g., Diet Coke in 1982), the firm's value rose from $4 billion, when he took the helm, to $145 billion in 1997, when he passed away while still serving as chairman.

Today, Coke is the world's number one soft-drink company by size, owning four of the top five soft-drink brands (Coca-Cola, Diet Coke, Fanta, and Sprite). The firm makes or licenses over 400 drink products in total, with distribution in over 200 countries. Although it does no bottling itself, Coke owns 35 percent of Coca-Cola Enterprises (the top Coke bottler in the world).

Ho Ho Coca-Cola

Coke is also responsible for shaping one of today's most iconic images: Santa Claus. Beginning in 1931, Coke started running ads in popular magazines featuring St. Nick as a jolly man with a white beard in a red suit. In prior years, various images of Santa circulated, some depicting him in different colored suits and minus the weight problem. These images began to fade once artist Haddon Sunblom went to work for Coke, painting pictures of Santa resembling the modern image we're now accustomed to seeing in movies and commercials. The Coca-Cola Santa made his debut in 1931 in *The Saturday Evening Post.*

Source: Hoover's, Inc.

Consumer Appliances Most goods deemed to be Consumer Staples are nondurable, meaning the products have short useful lives, and once they are used up, consumers normally buy more of the same product. Maintaining the supply of nondurable goods we commonly use today (like clothing and food) requires a variety of durable goods (like appliances). In the 1920s, several appliance inventions sprung up in most US households, including electric washing machines, dishwashers, vacuum cleaners, stoves, toasters, irons, and refrigerators. Without these appliances coming to market, the Food, Beverage, and Household Products industries would have evolved quite differently.

Take food, for example. Refrigerators enabled longer storage of perishables and dramatically shrank food preparation time. Whereas in prior decades an average American could spend an astounding 44 hours per week simply preparing and cleaning up after meals,[14] less preparation time was needed as households began to shift to more processed foods.

Previously, most food was prepared from scratch—peeling potatoes, plucking chickens, grinding coffee beans, and so on. In the

1920s, that all began to change as food manufacturers became better at streamlining production of canned and frozen foods that could now be stored in refrigerators. Not surprisingly, there was a proliferation of processed foods in the 1920s, including Wonder Bread, Yoo-Hoo, Reese's Peanut Butter Cups, Wheaties, and Velveeta Cheese.

Not only did refrigeration help consumers store foods and drinks, but it also allowed companies to transport foods and beverages over long distances by road or sea, propelling rapid growth among the leading food and beverage companies of the time.

Titans That Grew Up in the Twentieth Century: The Procter & Gamble Company

A candle maker named William Procter and soap maker named James Gamble joined forces in Cincinnati in 1837, forming the Procter & Gamble Company (P&G).

By 1859, P&G was already one of Cincinnati's largest firms, with sales topping $1 million. Big product wins in subsequent years included Ivory soap in 1879 and Crisco shortening in 1911. The Ivory marketing campaign was groundbreaking because it appealed directly to consumers (other product manufacturers focused efforts on retailers). Ivory was also one of the first products to inject moralism into advertising, promising to be "99.44% pure." Procter & Gamble continued innovative advertising in later years and was an early user of radio and television for mass advertising. In 1932, P&G sponsored daytime radio dramas and, in 1939, aired its first Ivory TV commercial.

The founders' families turned over management reins in 1930. Over the next 30 years, P&G became the largest US seller of packaged goods. Following years of research, P&G introduced key brands like Tide detergent in 1947, Crest toothpaste in 1955, and Head & Shoulders shampoo and Pampers diapers in 1961. The firm also actively acquired brands like Spic and Span in 1945, Folgers Coffee in 1963, and Gillette in 2005.

Today, P&G is a brand behemoth and the world's top maker of household products. Procter & Gamble continues to invest aggressively in building brand recognition, unseating General Motors as the top ad spender in 2005 with an annual advertising budget of over $4.6 billion.

Source: Hoover's, Inc.

MASS MARKETING AND MODERN CONSUMER PRODUCTS

Mass marketing evolved slowly during the latter part of the nineteenth century and early part of the twentieth century. Then World War II came along—a game-changing event that unleashed pent-up demand, propelled a new road system called highways, and helped facilitate a rapid rise in new types of electronic equipment.

Post World War II

During World War II, many US factories shifted production away from consumer goods to items needed in the war, like planes and rifles. As a consequence, supplies of consumer goods dwindled during those years. When the war ended and the soldiers returned home, the pent-up demand of accumulated wealth was suddenly unleashed.[15]

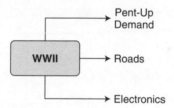

The war also influenced US roadways and electronics technology. While the US military was overseas during the war, top personnel became impressed with the German highway system. Germany had created the roadway to transport military personnel and goods quickly across the country. President Eisenhower embraced replicating the idea in the US and implemented the Interstate Highway System—roads connecting cities and burgeoning suburbs together. Research and development efforts (which boomed during the war to support the military's needs) also led to changes in electronics technology. Mass production methods also found their way into televisions and radios, making them affordable to average Americans.[16]

Mass Marketing Emerges

With the foundations in place from the war, massive consumer demand was met by massive stores and new forms of mass communication.

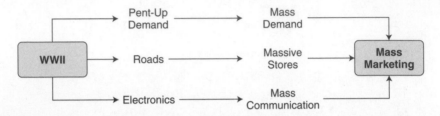

Soldiers returned home and the "baby boom" ensued—with lasting impacts on marketing ever since. Suburbs increasingly sprung up as highways made their way across the country, and with them, new malls and shopping centers. Televisions began to accompany radios in most homes, and consumerism in America underwent a fundamental shift once again. Mass marketing reached new heights.

As always, change brings opportunity. Procter & Gamble began producing television shows featuring their products, putting P&G, a manufacturer, directly in contact with millions of potential customers. This was a transformative shift, putting more power into the hands of product manufacturers while shifting power away from retailers, who previously possessed the only direct link with consumers. The era of mass marketing began to thrive, and consumer goods firms now had a medium to create any image they wanted to show to millions of consumers.[17]

Early Forms of Branding

The advent of mass marketing brought with it new management challenges that required strong centralized planning. It became common for consumer goods firms to organize their products into a form of divisional hierarchy, with individual brands at the bottom of the new organizational charts.

For instance, a firm like General Foods would have a coffee division. The coffee division would then be subdivided into various categories, such as the ground coffee group and the instant coffee group. Each of these groups would then have multiple brands (e.g., Maxwell House), and each brand would have an individual manager—a position now known as Brand Manager at most Staples companies. Given the mass orientation of the consumer products business, the brand managers began assuming responsibility over large marketing budgets, which were designed for mass advertising with a primary focus on television. Television shows were "bought" by advertisers for the whole year, and marketing departments churned out ads to run during the shows.[18]

Mass marketing was crucial in the evolution of corporate branding. Brand power is a central strategic attribute many Staples firms rely on to create perceived value—their well-respected name affords them the ability to price their products above the competition, and a loyal customer base will continually reuse their brands. There are many tools firms use to build their brand identities, including characters, logos, slogans, jingles, and unique packaging.

THE MODERN LANDSCAPE

An important lesson to learn from history is most all Consumer Staples goods were at one point in time discretionary—meaning some people bought and used them, some didn't. These goods weren't always firmly ingrained into the culture. Three ingredients were required for a consumer good to become a *staple*: mass production, mass marketing, and mass consumer adoption. Only through a combination of all these features could a good become truly homogenous with everyday life.

Another lesson: Although it seems odd to us now, people will one day look back at our modern Consumer Staples habits and view them as arcane—societal habits are always evolving. What doesn't change is the technology pendulum keeps swinging, and with new technology will come new customs. Our children and grandchildren will see amazing transformations take place in their futures. New production methods will evolve like we saw during the Industrial Revolution, new communication methods will change advertising (like we're seeing now with the Internet), and new shipping and travel technologies will increase the portability of both goods and consumers.

Will people still drink soda in 50 years or will soda be a relic of the past? Will people still smoke cigarettes? Will we discover that all the household cleaning products we use today have harmful chemicals that are banned someday? What will be the new Consumer Staples products of tomorrow that we can't even fathom today? Only time provides answers to these questions—we can only speculate.

Remember—lifestyles will change, just as they have in the past. Acknowledging this phenomenon helps combat our instinctual urge to always extrapolate forward present conditions. Anticipating change also gives you a better chance of noticing turning points when they come, no matter what sector you are following as an investor. The Consumer Staples sphere will continue evolving throughout our lifetime, and these changes will bring a continual string of new investment opportunities.

Chapter Recap

While history doesn't perfectly repeat itself, general patterns do tend to emerge. Understanding the past provides context for present affairs and future events. The consumer goods we consider "staples" of society today were not always so. In the US, there were several transformative periods in consumerism.

- Colonial America experienced a "Consumer Revolution," in which rising disposable income led to widespread adoption of a variety of consumer items that began to symbolize status and permeate everyday life (e.g., foods, beverages, beauty products).
- The advent of mass production techniques in the 1800s changed the consumer goods landscape as firms embraced economies of scale and produced greater quantities of goods at lower per-unit costs.
- Advancements in transportation allowed companies to increase their geographic distribution capacity while also facilitating greater mobility among consumers.
- Radio and television provided broadcast means for consumer product firms to advertise to large swaths of consumers simultaneously, propelling the formulation of distinctive brand identities.

3

CONSUMER STAPLES
SECTOR DRIVERS

In this chapter, we'll outline the most important macro drivers for the Consumer Staples sector. There are three categories of drivers you can use to examine the forward-looking prospects for any stock market sector. These include:

- Economic drivers
- Political drivers
- Sentiment drivers

We'll start by assessing the economic drivers most applicable to the Consumer Staples sector. While much of this discussion will center on the US, the principles can be applied to any country.

ECONOMIC DRIVERS

Macroeconomic indicators take the pulse of the economy. Whether it's jobs numbers, GDP, or the latest CPI report, these releases matter because to some degree they play a role in how most public companies perform. Astute investors follow macroeconomic data to gauge the current strength of the economy, as well as the direction it may head looking forward.

Deciphering economic data is not easy, however. The job is made difficult because many economic reports are volatile, contrast one another, and are subject to revision at a later date. Another problem with economic reports is they're not particularly useful on a short-term basis since the market discounts economic news with astounding speed.

So how do you use macroeconomic data to your advantage? You start by staying abreast of the most important indicators as they're released, constantly asking whether present conditions are better or worse than reflected by investor sentiment and market prices. Second, you formulate a rationale for where you think the economy may be heading in the future based on current trends. You're looking for predictive value. You're not as interested in what's on the cover of the *Wall Street Journal* today. You're interested in what's going to be on the cover next month or next year.

While a full book could easily be devoted to economic drivers, this section will focus on the macroeconomic drivers most applicable to the Consumer Staples sector. Specifically, we'll evaluate economic growth, interest rates, currency, and inflation. Understanding how these drivers impact the Consumer Staples sector will help you determine your relative portfolio allocation to the sector in different environments.

Economic Growth

The most straightforward economic driver is economic growth. The best way to measure economic growth is a country's gross domestic product (GDP).

What Is GDP?   There are four primary components to GDP:

1. Personal consumption expenditures: Consumer spending.
2. Gross private domestic investment: Business spending.

3. Government consumption expenditures and gross investment: Spending by federal, state, and local governments.

4. Net exports: The difference between goods *sold* by the US to foreigners and the goods *bought* by the US from foreigners.

US GDP measurements are released quarterly by the US Department of Commerce's Bureau of Economic Analysis (BEA—www.bea.gov).

GDP and Operational Performance   The top-line GDP figure is the final value of all goods and services produced in the US. But to understand what drives Consumer Staples stocks, you have to dig into the numbers. For instance, if GDP was much stronger than expected last quarter, ask: What were the reasons? Was it higher-than-expected government spending? Was there a big rebound in consumer spending? As a manager of a stock portfolio, determining the factors driving the broad economy is key to investing in appropriate areas of the market at optimal times.

Looking at the major components of GDP shown in Figure 3.1, the most influential to executives at Coke or Kimberly-Clark is what's

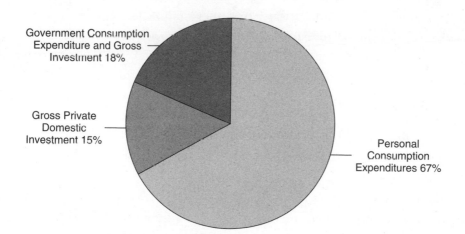

Figure 3.1   2007 GDP Breakdown
Source: Bureau of Economic Analysis.

happening with consumers. When GDP growth is announced, personal consumption expenditures are generally the first thing they look at.

Personal Consumption Expenditures *Personal consumption expenditures* (PCE), more commonly referred to as "consumer spending," account for about 70 percent of total GDP in the US. The PCE is a measure of total spending by consumers on goods and services. Because consumers play such a large role in the overall economy's health, analysts closely watch myriad other indicators like *disposable personal income* for clues on how consumers are faring.

Disposable income is income less taxes and indicates how much new money is available to an individual for spending and saving. Theoretically, the more disposable income people have, the more apt they are to buy goods and services. Therefore, PCE and disposable income are often pretty closely linked. Like PCE data, you can find disposable personal income figures on the BEA website.

As a Consumer Staples investor, your primary concern is not just how much consumers spend in aggregate. You must also try to distinguish what they're spending their money on. Three types of purchases fall into the PCE category of the GDP report: durable goods, nondurable goods, and services.

Nondurable goods is most relevant to Consumer Staples stocks. Nondurable goods possess a useful life of less than three years and include a wide variety of Staples items ranging from shampoo to batteries to vegetables. Some items classified as Consumer Discretionary products, like clothing, fit in here, too. The Consumer Staples sector is typified by products repeatedly bought by consumers in both good times and bad, so most Staples products constitute a nondurable good. Nondurables represent about 30 percent of all personal spending.[1]

PCE and Stock Performance Robust consumer spending generally has a positive effect on absolute performance for Consumer Staples stocks. Figure 3.2 shows the S&P 500 Consumer Staples sector's year-over-year (YoY) price change compared to the YoY change in nominal PCE.

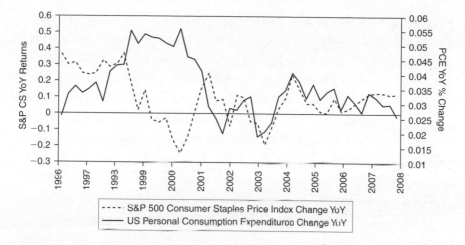

Figure 3.2   S&P 500 Consumer Staples Absolute Stock Performance vs. Nominal PCE Growth
Source: Thomson Datastream.

Figure 3.2 tells two stories. Consumer spending *generally* has a positive effect on absolute stock performance in the Consumer Staples sector, but that's not always the case—look at 1998 through early 2000. The Consumer Staples index experienced declining returns even though PCE grew at a healthy pace.

The foremost explanation for Consumer Staples' poor showing is likely investor euphoria accompanying the end of the raging 1990s bull market. In the late 1990s, many investors saw a high opportunity cost in tying up capital in Consumer Staples stocks, so they transferred investment dollars into more economically sensitive sectors like Tech. So even though most Staples firms were delivering strong operational performance because of robust consumer spending, investor sentiment was not in their favor on a relative basis, and returns suffered as a result.

The picture started changing in 2001, however, when investor euphoria started to give way and a bear market ensued. At this point, Staples stocks began to trade more in tandem with PCE, a trend that persisted from 2001 through 2007. This long-term relationship makes more intuitive sense—consumers spending more should help most Staples firms' bottom lines, which should eventually translate into stock performance. The correlation coefficient between PCE and absolute Consumer Staples performance in Figure 3.2 is 0.54, indicating a positive relationship between the two variables.

Time for a curveball. What if we switch things around and look at PCE versus *relative* Consumer Staples performance? Figure 3.3 presents the same PCE data, matched up against the Consumer Staples sector's relative performance to the S&P 500. This time we see a correlation coefficient of –0.65, conveying an inverse relationship. The graph shows the two variables traveling in opposite directions most of the time.

Similar to Figure 3.2, we see in Figure 3.3 that, from 1997 to 2000, Consumer Staples underperformed the broader market. Personal consumption expenditure was strong, the economy was strong, but investor sentiment was not in Consumer Staples' corner, so the sector grossly underperformed other areas of the market.

In 2000, the broad market slowed down, Tech stocks started to portend ominous signs, and Consumer Staples stocks' relative performance shot up. Notice this happened right when PCE began plummeting downward in early 2000. But if Consumer Staples

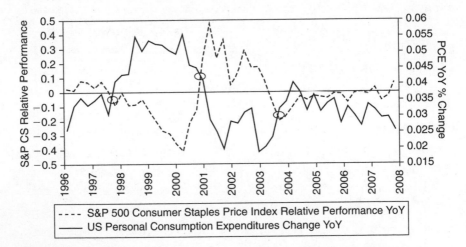

Figure 3.3   S&P 500 Consumer Staples Relative Stock Performance vs. Nominal PCE Growth
Source: Thomson Datastream.

businesses are positively driven by consumer spending, then why did the sector start to perform so well on a relative basis just when consumer spending started to fall off a cliff?

The answer lies in the role Consumer Staples stocks play in most investor portfolios—they are often considered a *defensive* safe haven. For this reason, it's important to clarify that the most powerful economic Staples driver, consumer spending, may have a *positive* correlation to revenue, earnings, and absolute stock performance, but it also tends to exhibit a *negative* correlation to relative stock performance.

The moral of the story: If you were going to own Consumer Staples stocks for the long term, you would probably see them perform better on an absolute basis when consumer spending and the economy are strengthening (just as you'd see the overall market perform better in such an environment). But if you're managing a diversified portfolio with the foremost goal of beating the market, you're more likely to achieve excess returns by owning more Consumer Staples stocks when consumer spending is weak and less when it's strong. Counterintuitive, but true.

Interest Rates

Interest rates are another important Consumer Staples driver because they signal borrowing costs for corporations and individuals.

When folks talk about *interest rates* they generally mean one of two categories. There's central bank interest rates—those controlled either directly or indirectly by a nation's central bank (in the US, it's the Federal Reserve or the "Fed"). These interest rates are used by central banks as one tool to enact monetary policy—raising or lowering them as they see appropriate to help moderate inflation, keep the economy moving, encourage employment, or achieve other policy ends.

All other interest rates—those on Treasuries of all maturities, corporate instruments, and other debt securities—are set by the market. These interest rates can and do move independently of central bank rates and are indicative of an entity's cost of borrowing.

Benign interest rates generally translate into lower borrowing costs, and higher interest rates make borrowing more expensive. Thus, a capital-intensive firm like Coca-Cola Enterprises (Coke's largest bottler) faces more headwinds from higher interest rates compared to a less capital-intensive firm like Coca-Cola Company (which owns the Coke brand but delegates a lot of the product manufacturing responsibilities).

In addition to impacting borrowing costs for corporations, interest rates can influence consumer behavior. Benign borrowing costs can create a favorable borrowing environment for individuals, which can lead to higher levels of PCE.

Currency

Currency affects operational results in two primary ways. First, a nation's weakening currency makes goods produced within that country relatively cheaper for overseas buyers. Cheaper prices abroad can act as a demand catalyst, helping boost revenues for firms selling abroad where currencies are stronger. When domestic currency strengthens, the opposite occurs, making a firm's goods more expensive for foreign consumers.

Not only can a weak currency make a domestic company's goods more competitive abroad, it can also lead to a positive effect from currency translation on the goods sold in countries with stronger currencies. For example, if Hershey's sells a bag of Reese's Pieces for $1 in the US and the same bag in Europe for €1, it will realize a foreign exchange benefit to its top-line revenue if the euro strengthens against the dollar. If the euro goes up 10 percent on the dollar and Hershey has not repatriated the euros received from the sale, Hershey can recognize revenue of $1.10 on its bag of Reese's. Of course, the opposite effect transpires when currencies where origin of sale occurs weaken in relation to domestic currency.

Currency can be an important variable in the Consumer Staples sector since many of the sector's bellwethers derive a large portion of sales overseas. Coca-Cola, for instance, derives more than 75 percent of its operating income from sales outside of North America.[2]

So while you needn't nail a currency forecast to choose a suitable investment, understanding a firm's currency exposure and how the firm manages it will leave you better equipped to analyze earnings drivers and risks.

Inflation

The third key macroeconomic Consumer Staples driver is inflation. There are several widely cited measures you can use to gauge inflation, including the Consumer Price Index (CPI) and the Producer Price Index (PPI).

What Is CPI? The Consumer Price Index reflects how much consumers pay for goods and services and is a widely used inflation indicator. The CPI measures inflation at the *retail* level. Specifically, the index measures the average change in retail prices over time for a basket of more than 200 categories of goods and services. The products included in CPI are organized into eight groups, demonstrated in Figure 3.4.

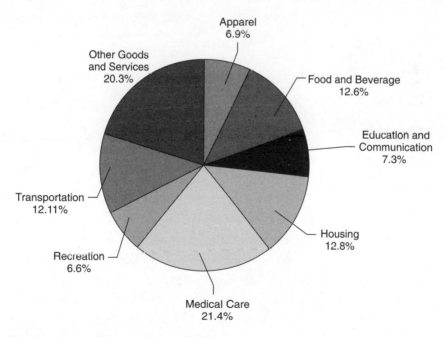

Figure 3.4   Slices of the CPI Pie
Source: Thomson Datastream, as of 6/30/2008.

The CPI is distributed monthly by the Bureau of Labor Statistics (BLS) and can be found at www.bls.gov. Note: CPI, like all government-produced economic statistics, has its inconsistencies and failings. But it does help paint a picture of overall consumer price trends.

CPI's Impact The BLS breaks down the eight CPI groups into greater detail. Take the food category, for example. The CPI classifies food into the "food at home" and "food away from home" sub-categories. These can be broken down further into individual products so you can see how prices are trending individually in meats, dairy, fruits, vegetables, and so on. All the major food groups are covered in CPI, as well as items from other Staples industries such as tobacco, alcoholic beverages, and personal care products.

Because of its expansive nature, the CPI report is a helpful resource to gauge pricing trends in the Consumer Staples sector. If the report shows a dramatic increase, it generally means retail prices are going up. Consumer Price Index going up can be a good thing for Staples firms since it results in higher unit sales. This kind of trend remains a positive as long as volumes sold stay consistent despite the price increases.

A drawback to CPI is that it doesn't tell you much about bottom-line performance. To gauge where margins might be trending, you need a more comprehensive view of the supply chain. The Producer Price Index (PPI) is a handy tool in this regard.

What Is PPI? While the CPI report measures inflation at the retail level, the PPI report measures inflation at the wholesale level. However, these two inflation gauges are linked to an extent because prices paid by businesses at the wholesale level usually foreshadow the prices retailers charge at the end of the supply chain.

The producer price series began in 1902, making it the country's oldest inflation measurement tool. To compute the report, the Labor Department sends questionnaires to nearly 30,000 firms regarding the pricing of 100,000 different items.[3] Essentially, the PPI report represents three indexes rolled into one, with each index representing goods at a different stage of the production process: the crude stage, intermediate stage, and finished product stage. The indexes are formally known as PPI Crude Goods, PPI Intermediate Goods, and PPI Finished Goods.

The PPI report is distributed monthly by the BLS (www.bls.gov).

PPI and Operational Performance To assess how PPI influences Staples stocks, we will evaluate each level of the supply chain. Theoretically, each level of PPI can be viewed as a leading indicator of the next level of PPI, starting with crude goods.

> **PPI Crude Goods**: The crude goods index represents the cost of raw materials, including food commodities, such as wheat and soybeans, and non-food commodities like coal and timber. Supply and demand drive prices in the commodity markets (as in all things traded in free markets). When demand outweighs supply, prices of crude goods rise, and input costs inflate for the basic ingredients in products consumed every day. Rising prices in this early part of the supply chain generally favor whoever is pulling the raw material out of the ground, be it a wheat farmer or a crude oil exploration company.

> **PPI Intermediate Goods**: As the second level in the PPI supply chain, much of intermediate goods pricing is based on what happens with crude goods. The intermediate goods index conveys the cost of commodities undergoing transitional processing prior to becoming a final product.

> Corn Products International, for instance, processes corn into corn syrup, which is later used in final products like soft drinks. If corn has gone up on the crude goods side of the PPI report, Corn Products, an intermediate firm, is likely to attempt to pass on its rising input cost by charging more for its corn syrup. This in turn affects Pepsi, whose products are found in the finished goods section of the PPI report.

> **PPI Finished Goods**: The finished goods index is the most closely watched aspect of the PPI report. Not only does it reference the final wholesale costs charged to retailers, but it also has the largest impact on prices consumers see when they go shopping.

If a retailer like Wal-Mart has to pay more for Pepsi products because Pepsi's input costs have gone up, it then has to decide how much room it has to pass on price increases to consumers. Since retailing is a very competitive landscape, pricing matters quite a bit, and competition often prohibits retailers from raising prices as much as the firms engaged in earlier stages of the production process. The different levels of pricing power in the supply chain mean producer prices do not delineate in linear fashion where consumer prices travel. If you notice a period when PPI rises more than CPI, producers are raising prices, but they're not being fully passed to the end customer. This can mean margin pressure is occurring with the retailers, who might be paying more for inventory but not raising prices at a commensurate level.

PPI Versus CPI   Figure 3.5 illustrates CPI and PPI trends since 1990, with PPI broken down into its three stages of production.

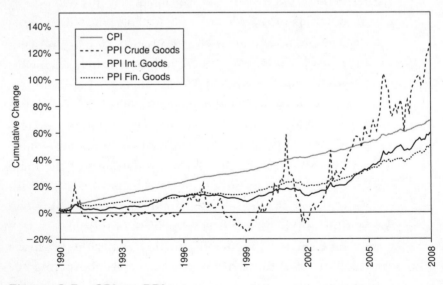

Figure 3.5   CPI vs. PPI

Source: Thomson Datastream.

Notice there is a similarity between CPI and PPI for finished goods since both rise at a steady pace. Meanwhile, producer prices at the crude level fluctuate wildly. Prices of raw materials can swing a lot because products in this sphere are commoditized. There's no one out there charging double everyone else for corn because they somehow have a superior brand—commodities are largely *fungible*. As you move through the supply chain to finished products, however, products become less standardized, brand power becomes more important, and premium pricing opportunities come into play.

The different layers of pricing power are what make the three levels of PPI look so different in Figure 3.5. Notice the sharp increase in crude goods since 2005, which has not been met by commensurate inflation in the intermediate or finished good categories. In 2008, many Consumer Staples executives were calling input cost pressure the worst they have seen in their 30-plus year careers.

However, despite the volatility associated with their input costs, firms engaged in finished products are not apt to adopt a volatile pricing strategy. Rather, they make very methodical pricing decisions based on their cost structure, their future outlook for commodities, and what their competitors are doing. This helps keep customers and market share consistent.

Consumer products account for approximately 75 percent of PPI Finished Goods, which makes it a useful indicator to reference when analyzing Consumer Staples stocks. If prices make a leap here, you can bet CPI will eventually follow, which means pricing power and brand quality are likely to become increasingly important strategic attributes as firms attempt to raise prices while maintaining volume growth.[4] Figure 3.6 breaks out the relative importance of the major categories of finished goods in the PPI index. The most relevant components to Consumer Staples include nondurable goods and consumer foods, which make up just over 64 percent of the pie.

Most investors interpret moderate inflation as healthy because it allows producers to charge more for goods, thereby bolstering revenues. There is no consensus on what the optimal inflation level is, however, so as an investor, you must continually analyze pricing and

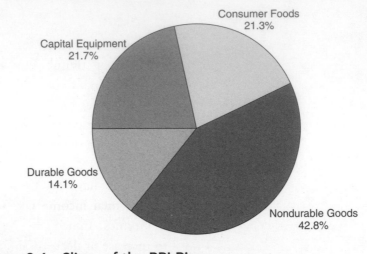

Figure 3.6   Slices of the PPI Pie
Source: Bureau of Labor Statistics, as of 12/31/2007.

volume trends in the Consumer Staples stocks you follow to understand how each individual business is coping with the present inflation conditions, whatever they may be.

You Always Pay For It

Raising prices is not the only way companies pass cost increases onto consumers.

Kellogg Co. has been successfully passing on soaring prices for ingredients and fuel to consumers by using smaller cereal boxes. Beginning in June 2008, Kellogg began rolling out Froot Loops, Cocoa Krispies, and Apple Jacks boxes weighing 2.4 ounces less in size, amounting to low- to mid-single-digit wholesale price increases.

Source: "Kellogg Shrinks Boxes, Passing Costs to Buyers," *Wall Street Journal* (June 16, 2008).

POLITICAL DRIVERS

What happens in Washington influences what happens on Wall Street. Always has and probably always will. So let's turn our attention to some of the political drivers most relevant to the Consumer Staples sector—taxes and trade policy.

Taxes

Tax policy is an ever-present driver of the stock market on both macro and micro levels. As a general rule of thumb, anything you increase taxes on you can expect to get less of. If you materially increase taxes on potato chips, people will likely eat fewer chips and switch to alternatives, like pretzels. Taxes are an important driver of overall economic activity and can also play a role in determining specific industry performance.

We can look at the aggregate effects taxes have on the economy through several lenses. First, there's personal income tax. John Maynard Keynes, father of Keynesian economics, argued the government could use taxes as puppet strings to increase or decrease society's consumption levels. The basis for the theory is that tax policy alters the level of disposable income for consumers. Lower taxes can be a boon to the economy based on the marginal propensity to consume.

For those of you who skipped Econ 101, *marginal propensity to consume* describes consumption changes in response to changes in disposable income. In equation form, it is equal to the change in consumption divided by the change in disposable income responsible for the consumption change. For example, if the Jones family gets a tax break and their household income goes up $10,000 this year, and their marginal propensity to consume is 0.70, they will spend $7,000 more this year while saving an extra $3,000. Through the *multiplier effect*, their $7,000 will be spent several times over by other parties involved in the economic chain, enhancing overall economic activity.

When changes in personal income tax policy occur, investors have to ask two questions: How will the change affect the economy, and which sectors are best poised to benefit?

Since higher levels of disposable income normally translate to higher consumer spending, and higher consumer spending is negatively correlated to Consumer Staples' relative performance (based on our earlier analysis), lower taxes may support the notion of underweighting the sector. Conversely, if you think higher taxes have the potential to detract from disposable income and slow down consumer spending, you might want to consider tax drivers as supportive reasoning for overweighting the sector.

The second major tax driver is sales tax. Sales tax is a point-of-sale consumption tax. When countries or states increase sales tax, consumer spending is inevitably affected, requiring an analysis similar to what you would conduct when assessing personal income tax changes.

In many overseas regions, including Europe, a value-added tax (VAT) system is prevalent. This tax system is different than sales tax in that VAT is levied on businesses as a fraction of the price of each taxable sale. Value-added tax is based on the total value added to goods at each level of the supply chain. End prices to consumers are still higher or lower depending on how high tax rates are, but they are absorbed by businesses at varying rates. For example, in Germany, VAT is split into two levels: VAT for food items and VAT for non-food items. Different rates could apply to each category and vary across the EU member states. Monitoring VAT provisions is a consideration when you are investing in international Consumer Staples firms because changes in VAT rates can affect both consumption and individual firms' profitability depending on where they operate.

The last important aspect to monitor in relation to taxes as a driver for Consumer Staples stocks is how they impact specific industries. Legislators have been known to target select Staples industries in an attempt to deter consumption of products deemed moral hazards, like cigarettes and alcohol. Since 1997, for example, the weighted average state tax in the US on cigarettes has gone up 198 percent— from $0.32 in 1997 to $0.95 in 2008.[5] A hypothetical example of a future tax that could impact the Staples sector would be a mandatory tax on sugary products, like soda, in an effort to fight obesity.

Trade Policy

Free trade is essential to globalization, opening up trade and capital flows across borders. But while the international community has become more integrated from a trade perspective, there are still unnatural forces finding their way into the market, distorting the natural pricing mechanism. These unnatural forces are mainly tariffs and subsidies.

Trade policy theoretically affects all Consumer Staples firms that export goods and those that own foreign subsidiaries. Countries maintain trade pacts with one another, and depending on the terms of the agreements, domestic producers may or may not be able to compete effectively in foreign markets. When the protectionist wind blows, governments may be inclined to increase subsidies for their domestic producers or enact tariffs on imported goods. Either of these actions alters the competitive landscape.

Nice Work If You Can Get It

If you're fond of the outdoors, being a US farmer has its perks. In 2004, US farm programs transferred $16.2 billion from US food consumers to producers through subsidies and tariffs. One can't help but question this type of "assistance," since US agricultural policies are essentially unchanged since the 1930s and the average income of farmers ($79,965 in 2005) exceeds that of the average US household ($63,344 in 2005).

Source: Chris Edwards, "Ten Reasons to Cut Farm Subsidies," Center for Trade Policy Studies (June 28, 2007); Daniel Griswold, "The High Price of Farm Policies," Center for Trade Policy Studies (September 25, 2005).

Trade policy is most influential in the Consumer Staples sector when you consider agriculture, which is easily the most distorted industry. Governments in developed countries provide large subsidies through price supports and direct payments to farmers. This handicaps developing countries, who frequently have a comparative advantage in agricultural products but cannot afford to subsidize their agricultural sectors. Furthermore, many developing countries face prohibitive tariffs for their products abroad. Farmers are a political force to be reckoned with and maintain powerful lobby groups, making reform politically difficult in developed regions like the US and the EU. Ultimately, subsidies and tariffs breed inefficiencies and result in higher prices for consumers.

SENTIMENT DRIVERS

Sentiment is the most intangible driver of the stock market. At its core, sentiment equates to the mood people are in. Sentiment can play a large role in stock market behavior because the stock market is driven by human beings making decisions—inclusive of their rationalities and irrationalities.

A Corny Dilemma

If you're intrigued, you might try growing corn. The US heavily taxes sugarcane ethanol imported from Brazil to keep it from competing with corn ethanol grown in the US. The tariff exists because if foreign ethanol were introduced at fair market value, the ethanol program at home would be undermined since corn-based ethanol is not as cheap to produce as ethanol derived from sugarcane, the standard in Brazil. Domestic corn farmers applaud the tariff because it pushes up corn prices by artificially stimulating demand. One Consumer Staples firm benefiting from this trade policy is Archer Daniels Midland (ADM), a grain processor that also happens to be the largest domestic ethanol producer.

While a firm like ADM has an incentive to welcome these tariffs, consumers have good reason to think twice. Results for consumers include paying more for ethanol, food, and anything else corn-related because of the government-imposed distortion of Brazil's comparative advantage.

Sentiment also plays a role in consumer behavior, like style trends in automobiles or clothes. Bellbottom jeans in the 1970s were a fabric of sentiment. For Consumer Staples products, sentiment weighs on the popularity of foods (e.g., when the Atkins Diet became popular, high-carbohydrate foods became unpopular), what types of beauty products are in vogue, and what types of beverage products become the next fad.

As an investor, the two primary sentiment drivers to follow in relation to the Consumer Staples sector on an ongoing basis include elastic or inelastic preferences and brand value.

Elastic/Inelastic Preference

Understanding whether sentiment is likely to favor price and income elastic or inelastic firms is a key variable in assessing the Consumer Staples weighting in your portfolio. When investor sentiment becomes bearish, investors traditionally place a premium on price and income inelastic companies deemed likely to see consistent demand independent of a deteriorating economic environment. During such periods, Consumer Staples stocks are likely to see an expansion in their relative valuation multiples. Conversely, when price and income elasticity become highly coveted attributes, Staples stocks see relative multiple contraction as investors favor more economically sensitive investments (like Tech in the late 1990s). Either way, the increase or decrease in relative valuation is largely the result of a sentiment shift.

Brand Value

Occasionally, the market places a heightened premium on intangibles, like brand value. In the 1990s, for instance, Coca-Cola was perceived to have an unstoppable global brand, leading to a P/E ratio above 40 (territory usually reserved for high-growth Tech stocks rather than Consumer Staples firms). Brand equity becomes a focal point when firms have to contend with rising input costs that necessitate price increases to consumers. When compared to firms with weak brands, firms with the strongest brands are most able to maintain their customer base while raising prices.

Chapter Recap

The Consumer Staples sector has a multitude of drivers that dictate both operational and stock market performance. These drivers can be grouped into three categories: economic, political, and sentiment.

- The most straightforward economic driver is economic growth, most commonly measured by gross domestic product (GDP).
- Consumer spending (PCE) is the most important component of GDP in relation to the Consumer Staples sector. The PCE exhibits a positive correlation to absolute sector performance and negative correlation to relative sector performance.
- Interest rates affect the cost of capital for Consumer Staples firms and impact consumer behavior.
- Currency movements affect revenues and profits for firms with international sales.
- Inflation is a driver of Consumer Staples stocks and is most commonly measured through the CPI and PPI indexes. The CPI illustrates retail price inflation, and PPI demonstrates inflation through the production phase. Analyzing each index separately provides clues to help understand input cost pressure and pricing trends in the sector.
- Political drivers such as taxes and trade policy also influence the Consumer Staples sector. Tax policy can impact demand levels for consumer products, while trade policy often plays a role in supply.
- Sentiment is the most intangible driver of the Consumer Staples sector. Specific sentiment drivers to monitor include elastic versus inelastic preferences and brand value.

II

NEXT STEPS: CONSUMER STAPLES DETAILS

4

CONSUMER STAPLES SECTOR BREAKDOWN

Now that you have a high-level understanding of the Consumer Staples sector and its origins, it's time to explore the industries that make up the sector. We'll cover each industry by asking four fundamental questions:

1. How big is the market?
2. Who are the biggest players?
3. How does the industry operate?
4. What are the industry drivers?

Answering these questions provides insight into the basic framework of each Consumer Staples industry. Armed with this knowledge, you can better understand the variables business managers in the sector grapple with day to day, which can make you a better Consumer Staples investor.

This chapter can serve as a reference guide to use when seeking a refresher on industries you may consider investing in. With that in mind, feel free to skip around if you're particularly interested in certain industries.

GLOBAL INDUSTRY CLASSIFICATION STANDARD (GICS)

Before beginning, some definitions: The Global Industry Classification Standard (GICS) is a widely accepted framework for classifying companies into groups based on similarities. The GICS structure consists of 10 sectors, 24 industry groups, 68 industries, and 154 sub-industries. This structure offers four levels of hierarchy, ranging from the most general sector to the most specialized sub-industry:

- Sector
- Industry Group
- Industry
- Sub-Industry

Let's start by breaking down the Consumer Staples sector into its different components. According to GICS, the Consumer Staples sector consists of three industry groups, six industries, and nine sub-industries. The following are Consumer Staples industries and corresponding sub-industries.

- Beverages
  - Brewers
  - Distillers & Vintners
  - Soft Drinks
- Food Products
  - Agricultural Products
  - Packaged Foods & Meats
- Tobacco
- Household Products
- Personal Products
- Food and Staples Retailing
  - Drug Retail
  - Food Distributors
  - Food Retail
  - Hypermarkets & Super Centers

But before delving deeper into the industries, it's vital to understand what Consumer Staples looks like globally and how it fits into a broader benchmark.

GLOBAL CONSUMER STAPLES BENCHMARKS

What's a benchmark? What does it do, and why is it necessary? A *benchmark* is your guide for building a stock portfolio. You can use any well-constructed index as a benchmark—examples are in Table 4.1. By studying a benchmark's (i.e., the index's) make-up, investors can assign expected risk and return to make underweight and overweight decisions for each industry. This is just as true for a sector as it is for the broader stock market, and there are many potential Consumer Staples sector benchmarks to choose from. (Benchmarks will be further explored with the top-down method in Chapter 7.)

Differences in Benchmarks

So what does the Consumer Staples investment universe look like? It depends on the benchmark, so choose carefully! The large-cap US Consumer Staples sector looks different from small cap, and emerging markets (EM) looks different from the developed world.

Why the large-cap and developed-world bias? Much of the difference can be attributed to the vast market share and international footprint many of the world's largest Staples firms possess. Developed-world firms are big sellers to emerging markets (helping explain the relatively small Staples weighting in EM). Successful small-cap Staples firms, meanwhile, are likely to be bought by the big guys, so there's some survivorship bias. Table 4.1 shows major domestic and international benchmark indexes and the percentage weight of each sector.

Table 4.1 shows the Consumer Staples sector comprises about 9 percent of the developed-world market (based on the MSCI World benchmark). Utilizing a global top-down investment strategy, you

Table 4.1   Benchmark Differences

Sector	MSCI World (Developed World)	MSCI EAFE (Developed World ex-US)	S&P 500 (Large-Cap US)	Russell 2000 (Small-Cap US)	MSCI Emerging Markets (Emerging Markets)
Consumer Discretionary	9.8%	10.8%	8.5%	13.5%	4.9%
Consumer Staples	8.8%	8.5%	10.2%	3.0%	4.2%
Energy	10.9%	7.9%	12.9%	6.7%	18.0%
Financials	22.6%	26.9%	17.6%	18.9%	21.7%
Health Care	8.7%	6.3%	12.0%	14.5%	1.6%
Industrials	11.4%	12.1%	11.5%	15.1%	9.7%
Information Technology	11.0%	5.5%	16.7%	18.3%	10.1%
Materials	7.2%	9.9%	3.3%	5.6%	14.7%
Telecommunication Services	4.9%	6.2%	3.6%	1.5%	11.5%
Utilities	4.7%	5.9%	3.6%	3.0%	3.5%
Total	100.0%	100.0%	100.0%	100.0%	100.0%

Source: Thomson Datastream; MSCI, Inc.[1] as of 12/31/07.

can use this percentage as a rough gauge for how much you should allocate toward Consumer Staples stocks in your portfolio. (Note: We will discuss in later chapters how to formulate more precise allocations based on your perception of market conditions.)

Knowing the benchmark sector weight is a helpful starting point, but there's a critical question left to answer—what kind of Consumer Staples stocks do you want to own? You can refine your search by looking at the industry breakdown of the sector, which we've demonstrated for the MSCI World in Figure 4.1.

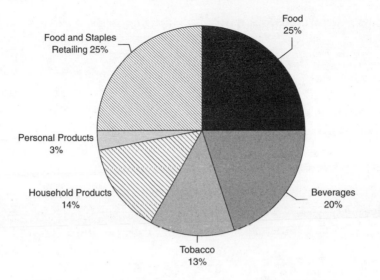

Figure 4.1   Industry Breakdown of the MSCI World Consumer Staples

Source: Thomson Datastream as of 12/31/2007.

FOOD, BEVERAGE & TOBACCO

And now, a look at the industries and sub-industries themselves. As we examine each industry (or sub-industry), we'll focus primarily on four factors:

1. Market size.
2. Biggest players.
3. Modes of operation.
4. Unique industry drivers.

Global Industry Classification Standard (GICS) groups the Food, Beverage & Tobacco industries together as one industry group. Food includes companies producing food products like cereal, microwave meals, and confectionary items like gum and candy. Beverage includes companies in the business of making things like carbonated soda, bottled water, spirits, and juices. The Tobacco industry is represented by the biggest cigarette manufacturers and doesn't have much in common with Food or Beverage other than their "staple" feature.

Because these industries are quite different, we'll break them down individually, starting with Food.

The Food Industry

Like many industries, there are upstream and downstream elements to the food business. Some Food firms are engaged in the early stages of processed food production and work closely with farmers to produce agricultural products. Later-stage firms take agricultural products and turn them into the finished packaged foods you find on grocery store shelves. The global Food Products industry is subdivided between just two sub-industries—Packaged Foods & Meats (comprising 92.4 percent) and Agricultural Products (comprising just 7.6 percent of the overall Food industry).

Just how big is the global Food market? Close to $1 trillion, representing about 25 percent of the MSCI World Consumer Staples benchmark.[2] Table 4.2 shows the 10 largest Food companies globally, listed by market capitalization.

Table 4.2   Ten Largest Global Food Companies

Rank	Company	Country	Market Cap (Millions)
1	Nestlé	Switzerland	$180,544
2	Unilever Group*	UK/Netherlands	$111,906
3	Kraft Foods	US	$50,485
4	Danone	France	$46,037
5	Archer Daniels Midland	US	$29,849
6	Cadbury	UK	$26,062
7	Wilmar International	Singapore	$23,911
8	Kellogg	US	$20,653
9	General Mills	US	$19,196
10	Heinz	US	$14,793

* Unilever Group is a dual listing of two parent companies: Unilever NV (Netherlands) and Unilever PLC (United Kingdom).
Source: Thomson Datastream, as of 12/31/2007.

Stay In or Go Out?

When analyzing the Food business, it is common to separate food purchased at the supermarket and consumed at home from food purchased at restaurants (or away from home). National food expenditures in the "at home" and "away from home" categories are profiled in Table 4.3.

Notice the increasing prevalence of Americans eating outside the home through the years. In 1960, 76 percent of food expenditures were on foods consumed at home. By 2006, this number shrank to 53 percent. Since family meals around the dinner table have become less frequent, food manufacturers have responded with an increasing number of products that can be consumed "on the go," like protein bars, snack packs, and microwave meals.

Table 4.3   US Spending on Food Products*

Year	At Home	Away from Home	Total
2006	546.9	486.2	1,033.1
2005	515.1	451.6	966.6
2004	487.4	427.0	914.4
2003	468.6	403.9	872.4
2002	450.0	385.2	835.3
2001	437.8	369.5	807.4
2000	416.0	357.2	773.3
1995	342.1	276.5	618.7
1990	296.8	225.3	522.1
1980	179.7	103.1	282.8
1970	74.8	33.8	108.6
1960	50.3	16.2	66.5

* All amounts in billions of dollars.
Source: US Department of Agriculture.

Agribusiness   The Food industry can be further segmented in the way it operates—agribusiness versus the packaged food business. The Food industry starts at the farm. Farms produce commodities supplied to meat and crop processing companies, known as agribusinesses.

Agribusinesses find themselves in the middle stages of the food production process, halfway between the farmer and the supermarket.

Crop processors produce ingredients sold to food packagers, who create finished products. Examples of crop-processing companies include Archer Daniels Midland Co. and Bunge Limited. These companies process raw grains, including corn, wheat, and soybeans. Their finished products include things like oils, starches, and corn syrup.

A Bumper Crop of Corn

Corn is the largest US crop in terms of acres harvested. Its popularity is not just due to people liking corn on the cob. There are more than 3,500 different uses for corn, mostly in consumer- and industrial-related products. Common uses include livestock feed, starch, ethanol fuel, and a variety of oil products.

Source: Corn Refiners Association; Mica Rosenberg, "Mexico Approves Rules To Begin Planting GM Corn," *Planet Ark* (March 25, 2008).

Meat processors also play a middleman role. These firms engage in slaughtering and processing livestock in preparation for retail sale. Life cycles vary among different livestock animals, affecting how nimble the respective supply chains are. Chickens and turkeys, for instance, are the quickest to raise and bring to market (their life cycles average around seven months). Even though many meat processors are middlemen, others, such as Hormel Foods, are vertically integrated. Hormel raises and slaughters its own hogs and also sells end-products like Spam and Hormel Chili.

The final agribusiness is dairy, which includes firms producing things like milk, butter, and cheese. Over the years, dairy farmers have become increasingly dependent on automated processes in their production, diminishing their reliance on human labor. This has propelled scale advantages, leading to some consolidation in what is still a very fragmented industry. The largest consolidator in the dairy production industry is Dean Foods.

Distribution is vitally important in agribusiness since most of these companies ship their products great distances to food processors or retailers. They rely on various modes of transportation to do so, including trucks, railroads, and ship barges. Food-processing giant Archer Daniels owns and operates over 20,000 rail cars, 1,500 tractor-trailers, and 2,000 barges.[3]

Packaged Food Business   Firms involved in the late stages of the food production business are known as *Packaged Food* companies. Firms like Kraft Foods and Kellogg's sell finished goods to retailers, who sell them to you. Getting food from the processing stage to the retailer is where most of the total cost of food is derived. Packaged Food firms pay to package the products, transport them to the retailer, and advertise them for sale. Personnel costs are a heavy component for Packaged Food companies because they pay high salaries to attract managerial talent capable of growing the company's brands.

Packaged Food firms have various distribution channels. Some companies transport products directly to retail stores and stock the shelves themselves. Other firms might have warehouse operations, where they store their products until the retailer or a third party picks them up for transport to a store.

The most important retail channel for the "at home" food category is grocery stores. Recently, supercenters and warehouse clubs have played an increasingly prominent role as firms like Wal-Mart have moved more into food sales. In an effort to improve distribution capabilities and better target the "away from home" food category, firms such as HJ Heinz and Campbell Soup Co. are selling through "food service outlets" (retail locations other than supermarkets). Firms are also expanding distribution overseas into rapidly growing markets.

To help you understand how these different supply chain structures translate to the bottom line, Tables 4.4 and 4.5 show the five largest global agribusinesses and Packaged Food companies, along with their five-year operating margin average. Notice the Packaged Food firms have higher margins. This is primarily because their end products are more clearly differentiated to the consumer, whereas the output of grain processors is more commoditized. In general, the more commoditized your product, the less margin you are likely to

Table 4.4   Five Largest Global Agribusiness Firms

Rank	Company	Country	Market Cap (millions)	Operating Margins (5Y Avg.)
1	Archer Daniels Midland	US	$29,849	4.0%
2	Wilmar Intl.	Singapore	$23,911	6.0%
3	Bunge	US	$14,079	2.9%
4	Südzucker	Germany	$4,482	8.5%
5	Danisco	Denmark	$3,469	10.9%

Source: Thomson Datastream as of 12/31/2007, Bloomberg Finance L.P.

Table 4.5   Five Largest Global Packaged Foods & Meats Firms

Rank	Company	Country	Market Cap (millions)	Operating Margins (5Y Avg.)
1	Nestlé	Switzerland	$180,544	13.0%
2	Unilever Group*	Netherlands/UK	$111,906	14.3%
3	Kraft Foods	US	$50,485	15.1%
4	Danone	France	$46,037	13.2%
5	Cadbury	UK	$26,062	13.8%

* Unilever Group is a dual listing of two parent companies: Unilever NV (Netherlands) and Unilever PLC (United Kingdom). Operating margin calculated based on the weighted average of the two respective companies.
Source: Thomson Datastream as of 12/31/2007, Bloomberg Finance L.P.

command. This is because undifferentiated products have no basis for premium pricing power. It's important to note that agribusinesses are hypersensitive to changes in commodity prices and can sometimes trade more like Materials stocks than Consumer Staples.

Food Industry Drivers   People need to eat in order to live. Pretty basic. In that respect, the Food industry enjoys a higher fixed level of demand than just about any other industry. But that doesn't mean demand in the Food industry never changes. There are several secular drivers that play a role in the Food business, independent of the economic cycle.

Population Growth. The easiest long-term industry driver to diagnose is population growth—the more people, the more mouths to feed. In this respect, both agribusinesses and Packaged Food companies benefit from rising populations and purposefully seek expansion in countries with the strongest population growth outlooks.

Wealth. The wealthier people are, the more food they will consume (up to some limit, of course). This trend is taking shape in parts of the developing world, where food demand has risen substantially simply because there are a lot more people now eating two meals a day instead of one.

Household wealth plays a different role in the developed world. Rather than eating a lot more food, citizens of developed countries are more likely to eat higher quality food, which usually means upgrading to more expensive brands. Food companies relish a trade-up effect because it fosters higher margins.

Shifting Consumer Preferences. Although population growth and wealth are big-picture drivers in overall food demand, there are also changing seasonal drivers. The foremost driver has to do with shifting consumer preferences. Today, consumers want it all in the food products they buy—taste, health benefits, and convenience. Some examples of how this impacts producers are listed in the nearby box.

Demographic Shifts. Demographics are an important demand catalyst across the Consumer Staples sector, including the Food business. Immigration is creating larger ethnic groups for Food companies to target. Most important to this trend is the current Hispanic population of 44 million, which is growing more rapidly than any other group in the US. Along with population growth, demand growth in the $5.7 billion Hispanic foods market is likely to accelerate—the Census

Those Fickle Consumers

Here are just a few examples of how Food firms have responded to consumers' changing preferences:

- Aging boomers are fighting rising blood pressure by reducing salt intake.
  - Campbell's capitalized on this by introducing reduced sodium soup, the top-selling new food product of 2007, bringing in over $100 million in sales in its first year.
- Years ago, no one ate chocolate or chewed gum for nutritional value, but times are changing.
  - In 2008, candy giant Mars (a private company) rolled out a Dove label called "Beautiful"—a chocolate featuring skin-nourishing additives like vitamins C and E, biotin, and zinc. The chocolate promises to "help hydrate from within to support beautiful-looking skin."
  - Wrigley and other gum makers are rolling out functional products with features like antioxidants and teeth-whitening additives.
- Those watching their weight can nibble portion-control snacks like Frito-Lay Mini Bites, Hershey's 100-calorie candy packs, and Quaker Chewy 90 Calorie Granola Bars. The value proposition is "indulgence without calories." For those cutting sugar, confectionary firms like Hershey's are rolling out new sugar-free versions of candy classics like Twizzlers and Jolly Rancher.
- According to a joint study by the Natural Marketing Institute and The Nielsen Co., about 20 percent of Americans include organics and other "green" products in their diets. Whereas Whole Foods has always sold organics, traditional supermarkets like Kroger and Safeway are just now creating their own organic store sections.

Source: Diane Toops, "The Year's Top-Selling Food Products," FoodProcessing.com; Marcia Mogelonsky, "Sugar-Free Foods and Beverages," PreparedFoods; Betsy Cummings, "Despite Economic Dip, Organic Food Sales Soar," *BrandWeek* (June 8, 2008).

Bureau estimates Hispanic buying power will exceed $1 trillion by 2011.[4]

Foreign Markets. Food is a mature industry in the US, with consumption growth rising a mere 1 percent annually. Consequently, domestic food companies welcome burgeoning overseas demand. Economic gains are transforming societies at breakneck speeds in emerging markets and facilitating a rapid increase of the middle class in many countries. For example, the World Bank estimates that by 2030, more than 600 million people in East Asia will earn enough to be considered middle class, up from about 100 million in 2000. With increasing incomes, citizens of these countries are seeing higher standards of living, which include consumption of western foods and beverage products.

Supply Drivers. Food supply starts at the agricultural level, where common inputs include seeds, fertilizer, weed control chemicals, fuel, and electricity. Agricultural technology is an important factor in the Food industry. New strains of genetically modified seeds have emerged, along with improved fertilizers and chemicals for controlling weeds and pests. Farm machinery has enhanced seed planting and threshing and facilitated an easier transfer of grains and oilseeds to silos and elevators. New GPS guidance technologies have also benefited farmers. Combined, these advancements have improved crop yields and benefited supply.[5]

Weather is another important supply driver, playing a pivotal role in dictating crop sizes. Although weather is fairly unpredictable, commodity traders closely watch forecasts for the most important agricultural regions and trade accordingly.

Competition for resources also comes into play when dealing in agricultural commodities. When competition increases for a particular resource, supply shrinks and prices go up. Today's best example of competition for resources impacting food supply and pricing is in biofuels. Recent to the writing of this book, the World Bank leaked a report citing biofuels as responsible for 75 percent of the increase in crop prices from 2002 to 2008.[6] Since ethanol consumed 14 percent of the US corn crop in 2005, 19 percent in 2007, and is projected to account for over 30 percent of demand by 2009,[7] it's little wonder many blame biofuels for much of the food inflation experienced in 2008.

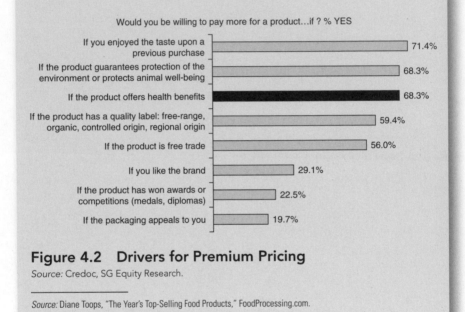

Taste Is Tops

Despite the rising preference for functional benefits from food, taste remains the most important food feature.

Chicago-based Information Resources Inc. (IRI) has tracked consumer packaged goods (CPGs) introductions for 13 years and found consumers still allocate two-thirds of their snack spending to the non-healthy stuff. Simply put, taste still matters most. Figure 4.2 illustrates how health benefits stack up against taste in a recent survey that looked at what qualities made consumers most apt to pay more for a food product.

Would you be willing to pay more for a product…if ? % YES

If you enjoyed the taste upon a previous purchase	71.4%
If the product guarantees protection of the environment or protects animal well-being	68.3%
If the product offers health benefits	68.3%
If the product has a quality label: free-range, organic, controlled origin, regional origin	59.4%
If the product is free trade	56.0%
If you like the brand	29.1%
If the product has won awards or competitions (medals, diplomas)	22.5%
If the packaging appeals to you	19.7%

Figure 4.2   Drivers for Premium Pricing
Source: Credoc, SG Equity Research.

Source: Diane Toops, "The Year's Top-Selling Food Products," FoodProcessing.com.

The Beverages Industry

The Beverages industry can be divided into three sub-industries: Soft Drinks (53 percent of the industry), Brewers (30 percent), and Distillers & Vintners (17 percent).[8] For the purposes of this chapter, we'll break down the beverage universe into non-alcoholic (Soft Drinks) and alcoholic beverages (Brewers and Distillers & Vintners).

The overall global Beverage industry is valued around $800 billion and represents about 20 percent of the MSCI World Consumer

Table 4.6 Ten Largest Global Beverage Companies

Rank	Company	Country	Market Cap (Millions)
1	Coca-Cola	US	$141,825
2	PepsiCo	US	$122,176
3	Diageo	UK	$55,771
4	InBev	Belgium	$51,233
5	SABMiller	UK	$42,428
6	Anheuser-Busch	US	$38,409
7	Heineken	Netherlands	$31,677
8	Pernod Ricard	France	$25,336
9	Coca-Cola Hellenic	Greece	$15,741
10	Kirin Holdings	Japan	$14,462

Source: Thomson Datastream, as of 12/31/2007.

Staples benchmark.[9] Table 4.6 illustrates the 10 largest global Beverage companies, ranked by market capitalization.

Non-Alcoholic Beverages   The non-alcoholic beverage category is diverse, representing soft drinks, sports drinks, energy drinks, bottled water, and any other packaged beverage product. As Table 4.6 shows, soft drink manufacturers remain the most dominant players in the space.

Franchise companies such as Coca-Cola or Pepsi-Cola have two central assets: their brands and their proprietary cola formulas. The primary function of these two rivals is to manufacture and sell their concentrates to licensed bottlers, who then sell and distribute the end product with some marketing support from the brand owner. In addition to supplying existing concentrates, both companies are active in developing new products and packaging while also running national marketing programs to support their respective brands. Since their primary function is marketing, few fixed assets are required, leading to high gross margins and returns on investment.

Bottlers typically combine the brand owner's concentrate with sweeteners and carbonated water, then package the drink in bottles

or cans to sell to wholesalers or retailers. They generally occupy desig-
nated territories and often handle the brand owner's fountain accounts
at restaurants, stadiums, and other public venues. Bottlers have higher
capital and labor cost burdens than the franchise companies. The
major bottlers include Coca-Cola Enterprises, Pepsi Bottling Group,
and Cott Corp. There are several common distribution channels tar-
geted by bottlers—referred to in the industry as *channel mix*. The primary channels for beverages include supermarkets, vending machines,
convenience stores, and fountain accounts.

Alcoholic Beverages   The Alcoholic Beverages industry is segmented into two more sub-industries—Brewers and Distillers &
Vintners. Brewers produce and distribute beer, which begins with
grains and hops. Some of the most commonly known beers, such
as Budweiser, are also brewed with rice. While the basic brewing
process is fairly uniform across companies, the level of vertical integration is not. Anheuser-Busch is the most vertically integrated—it has
an agricultural subsidiary that farms important grain ingredients and a
subsidiary that manufactures its cans.

Brewers own their plants and control manufacturing of their
products, so beer production tends to be capital intensive. Similar
to soft drink franchises, the major beer companies heavily emphasize
brand equity building through marketing.

Did You Know?

Anheuser-Busch is the number one purchaser of rice in the US, accounting for about 8
percent of total rice consumption.

Source: Standard & Poor's Industry Surveys: Alcoholic Beverages & Tobacco.

The Distillers & Vintners sub-industry covers the wine and spirits
makers. Wines vary foremost by the type of grapes used. According to
purchase agreements, big wine companies buy grapes from an array of
suppliers each year, hedging the risk of a poor harvest on a single sup-
plier. Once obtained, the grapes are crushed at company facilities and

stored as wine, which is generally sold within 18 months. In America, wine is distributed through wholesalers or state-level alcoholic agencies. Margins for vintners depend on scale and degree of vertical integration.

Distilled spirits manufacturers buy grains from farmers and mash them at their company distilleries. Products are aged over different periods. Similar to wine, they are distributed through wholesalers or state-level alcoholic beverage control agencies. Spirits are categorized as white goods (e.g., vodka), brown goods (e.g., whiskey), and specialties (e.g., cognac).

Beverages and the Income Statement The amount of alcohol isn't the only difference between major beverage industries. Some are more capital intensive than others. These variations result in differing margin characteristics, evident when comparing beverage firms' income statements.

We can see how the different operational structures in the Beverage industry translate to a profit and loss statement in Figure 4.3, which shows income statement characteristics of an assortment of Beverage firms. With the lowest cost structure of the group, franchise soft drink manufacturers possess the best profit margins and returns on investment (ROI) in the Beverage universe. For this reason, Coca-Cola and Pepsi-Cola normally trade at premium stock valuations to bottlers.

	Soft Drink Makers			Alcoholic Beverages			
	Franchiser	Bottler	Private Label	Domestic Brewer	Wholesaler	Vintner	Distiller
Net Revenue/Case	$0.90	$4.50	$1.80	$7.60	$12.80	$20–$50	$100
		(192 oz cases for soft drinks)		(288 oz cases)		(9L cases)	(9L cases)
Income Statement							
Revenue	100%	100%	100%	100%	100%	100%	100%
COGS	(30%)	(50%–55%)	(90%)	(55%–65%)	(75%)	(55%–80%)	(35%–80%)
Gross Profit	70%	45%–50%	10%	35%–40%	25%	20%–45%	20%–65%
Operating Costs	(35%)	(30%–35%)	(2%)	(10%–25%)	(15%–20%)	(5%–30%)	(5%–20%)
EBITDA	35%	15%	8%	10%–30%	(5%–10%)	15%–40%	15%–45%
D&A	(<5%)	(5%)	(2%)	(5%)	n/a	(5%–15%)	(5%–10%)
EBIT	30%	10%	(5%–10%)	5%–25%	n/a	10%–25%	10%–35%
ROI	25%–30%	5%–10%	5%–10%	10%–20%	n/a	5%–15%	5%–15%

Figure 4.3   Beverage Industry Profit & Loss Characteristics
Source: Goldman Sachs Research.

Did You Know?

Even though Coca-Cola Company and its bottlers are separate companies, they are still intimately tied to one another. Coke maintains equity investments of between 20 and 35 percent in affiliates like Coca-Cola Enterprises, Coca-Cola HBC, and Coca-Cola Amatil. The financial results of these equity method investments are reported as a one-line, non-operating item entitled "Equity income-net" on the Coca-Cola Company and Subsidiaries Consolidated Statement of Income.

Beverages Industry Drivers—Non-Alcoholic People are thirsty, creating a high level of fixed demand in this industry as well. Preferences and capacity to consume are less fixed, changing over time and dependent on a variety of drivers.

> **Population Growth.** Like the Food industry, population growth is a driver for beverage consumption. Expanding regions have higher numbers of new potential consumers.
>
> **Wealth.** Wealthier consumers in the US are more likely to buy premium beverage brands. Conversely, when the economy contracts, domestic consumers become less wealthy and are more likely to trade down in brand caliber.
>
> Wealth has an even greater impact on beverage consumption in many foreign markets. The US is a relatively mature beverage market—commercially sold beverages already comprise a robust 85 percent of liquid consumption in the US, compared to only 25 percent abroad. However, that 25 percent is growing rapidly, fueled by economic growth. Goldman Sachs recently conducted a study analyzing the variability of Coke's unit growth tied to global GDP. Their study demonstrates that robust GDP growth is a demand stimulus, prompting more people to drink carbonated soft drinks.
>
> **Innovation.** Innovation in the non-alcoholic beverage category usually entails things like new products with unique functional

Table 4.7   US Beverage Consumption

Type of Drink	2005 Market Share (%)	2006 Market Share (%)	% Change
Carbonated soft drinks	52.9	50.9	−2.0
Bottled water	26.1	27.8	1.7
Fruit beverages	14.3	13.5	−0.8
Sports drinks	4.2	4.5	0.3
Ready-to-drink tea	1.9	2.4	0.5
Energy drinks	0.5	0.8	0.3
Ready-to-drink coffee	0.1	0.1	0.0
Total	100	100	

Source: Beverage Marketing Corp.

benefits (e.g., VitaminWater), new flavors for existing products, unique packaging, and novel advertising campaigns.

Shifting consumer preferences. US carbonated soft drink volumes, which previously grew between 3 to 5 percent in the 1990s, are now on the decline, falling 2.3 percent in 2007. Soda is losing ground to alternatives such as bottled water, sports drinks, and energy drinks.[10] These new beverages appeal to consumers with increasingly busy lifestyles, as well as greater societal emphasis toward physical fitness and health. Soft drinks, on the other hand, have been linked with obesity by some reports. Table 4.7 shows US consumption of various beverage categories with a peek at the year-over-year changes from 2005 to 2006.

Distribution. Distribution and shelf space are important Beverage industry drivers. Large companies have innate advantages because they can easily work new drinks into their distribution chain. For example, if Pepsi wants to start selling a new drink, they can just put that new product on the truck that's already delivering Pepsi's core products to stores nationwide. This makes distribution of new products much easier for large firms than smaller firms, which have to invest more to facilitate distribution of a new product. Furthermore, securing shelf space is easier for larger firms that have pre-existing relationships with retailers.

Beverages Industry Drivers—Alcoholic   Though in the same industry, drivers can and do differ for alcoholic and non-alcoholic producers and distributors, so it's critical to consider them separately.

Population. With a population of over 1.3 billion people, China has been an attractive place for brewers seeking expansion. In 2003, China was estimated to be the largest consumer of beer in the world; and in 2005, it consumed over 30 million tons (more than 20 percent of the world market).[11] China's population size has helped make it the eighth-largest wine market, even though the country's per capita consumption rate is the lowest among the top 15 wine-consuming nations.[12]

Wealth. Increases in alcoholic beverage consumption in emerging countries like China remain mostly an urban phenomenon. Attracted by the huge numbers of jobs created by the economic boom, the workforce surging into large cities is driving sales of alcoholic beverages. The quality of products consumed is related to disposable income fluctuations. For example, as China's economy improved in the first half of the 1990s, consumers traded up in beer brands. As the economy continued to expand later in the decade, consumers once again traded up to still higher priced wines and spirits.

Innovation. Brewers have recently rolled out several new innovations to spur demand. Innovation in the alcoholic beverage world usually comes in two forms: flavors and packaging. Recent examples include SABMiller's successful 2007 launch of Miller Chill, a lime and salt lager, and Molson Coors' unique new packaging for Coors Light Cold Activated Bottles (the label's white lettering turns blue when the beer reaches optimal drinking temperature).

Shifting Consumer Preferences. Reduced-calorie beers began to grow in popularity in the 1980s while fuller flavored brews declined, giving rise to a proliferation in "light beers." Today, four of the top five beers in the US are light beers.

Microbrews have gained in stature in recent years as consumers gravitated toward more exotic tastes. Microbrews typically use 100 percent malted barley rather than the less expensive grains common to the mass-produced, US-style beers. Since 1992, the imported beers market has experienced double-digit annual growth, significantly outpacing the overall domestic category.[13] Mexican beers dominate the import category (47 percent of total 2007 imports). The biggest Mexican importer is Grupo Modelo, owner of the Corona and Pacifico brands.

Wine has become an increasingly tough competitor for beer in recent years. Wine marketers have positioned their products as part of an upper-class lifestyle, often summoning pictures of bucolic vineyards and sophisticated people pairing their wine with upscale cuisine. In a 2005 Gallup Poll, wine edged out beer as the preferred beverage for the first time in the history of the poll.[14]

Demographics. Wine and spirits consumers tend to be older, and the aging population in the US has been a driver for those beverage producers. As baby boomers age, they will likely continue bolstering demand for spirits and wine. In contrast, the millennial generation (21 to 30 year olds) has shown a preference for beer, particularly for imports and microbrews.

Foreign Markets. The brewing business has few truly international brands. Of the top 10 best-selling global brands, only Heineken derives a vast proportion of its sales internationally. Times are changing, however, as beer companies have become increasingly focused on building international distribution in fast-growing markets where they currently have low penetration rates. Two of the hottest beer markets currently are

Russia and China, who did not have access to foreign brands until recently.

One of the reasons China has been an attractive place for brewers to seek expansion is because per capita beer consumption is only 25 liters. This compares to 81 liters in the US, 97 in the UK, and 123 in Germany. Per capita beer consumption in China is still a long way from Germany, but it has been growing at a swift pace, quadrupling since 1990.[15]

Consolidation. Mergers between firms from different countries have become a more routine way to acquire distribution in new markets where firms have weak spots. Most prominently, the two largest global beer companies, InBev and Anheuser-Busch, agreed to a deal in 2008. The Belgian brewer sees vast potential in Anheuser-Busch for several reasons. First, Bud fixes InBev's lack of meaningful penetration into the US—and vice versa, since only 5 percent of Anheuser-Busch's beer is sold internationally. InBev has strong distribution channels in many of the developing markets that Bud has been unsuccessful in penetrating. The way InBev's CEO, Carlos Brito, sees it, people in developing countries are hungry for American brands, and he can bring them. "Consumers like the US lifestyle," he says, adding he can sell "America in a bottle."[16]

Other recent large mergers in the beer industry include America's number two and number three brewers joining forces in 2007 with the combination of SABMiller and Molson Coors, and Amsterdam-based Heineken and Copenhagen-based Carlsberg's joint takeover of Britain's Scottish & Newcastle in 2008.

The Tobacco Industry

As covered in Chapter 2, tobacco is one of America's oldest products. In the 1800s, most chewed tobacco or smoked it in a pipe. Cigarettes didn't become the preferred tobacco product until the early 1900s.

Today's global Tobacco industry is valued at around $400 billion and represents about 13 percent of the MSCI World Consumer

Which Is Your Favorite?

The world's top 10 beer brands ranked by 2007 sales volume are:

1. Bud Light (US)
2. Snow (China)
3. Budweiser (US)
4. Skol (International)
5. Corona (Mexico)
6. Heineken (Netherlands)
7. Brahma (Brazil)
8. Coors Light (US)
9. Miller Lite (US)
10. Tsingtao (China)

Source: Plato Logic; Jenny Wiggins, "Thirst to Be First: Race for a Global Lead in Beer," *Financial Times* (July 23, 2008).

Table 4.8   Five Largest Global Tobacco Companies

Rank	Company	Country	Market Cap (millions)
1	Altria Group	US	$159,196
2	British American Tobacco	UK	$78,919
3	Japan Tobacco	Japan	$59,795
4	Imperial Tobacco	UK	$36,574
5	Reynolds American	US	$19,458

Source: Thomson Datastream, as of 12/31/2007.

Staples benchmark.[17] The Tobacco industry is very concentrated, with five key players globally. Table 4.8 shows the five largest tobacco companies by market capitalization.

In terms of operations, the early stages of today's tobacco production haven't changed much over the centuries. Tobacco leaves are grown by farmers located mainly in the southeastern US. Tobacco farmers sell their leaves to dealers at public auctions. The dealers are paid commissions and act as middlemen between the farmer and the manufacturer. They process, pack, and store the tobacco before turning it over to manufacturers. Although manufacturers could also buy tobacco straight from the farmers, most prefer to work with dealers to avoid the capital- and labor-intensive business of tobacco processing, which allows them to focus on marketing the finished product (note this relationship is somewhat similar to soda franchises and their relationships with bottlers).

Once the manufacturer has secured the tobacco leaves, the tobacco is processed to create finished cigarettes. The end product is then distributed through wholesalers, large retailers, and vending machine operators. International distribution is often handled through export sales organizations.

A Tobacco Guarantee

From 1933 to 2004, the US had a price support system in place for tobacco farmers. A production quota was created to guarantee farmers minimum prices. This led to higher domestic cigarette prices than elsewhere in the world. The American Jobs Creation Act of 2004 eliminated the quotas and the price support system. Lower production prices should be beneficial to cigarette companies' operating margins and stimulate demand over time.

Tobacco Industry Drivers   The Tobacco industry is largely driven by the highly addictive nature of the products, resulting in a number of pros and cons. The pros include abnormally high pricing power, and the cons mostly surround negative health effects.

Price Increases Offset Volume Declines. Annual cigarette consumption fell by an average of 1.9 percent from 1994 to 2003. In recent years, volume declines slowed slightly, falling 1.1 percent in 2005 and 1.3 percent in 2006.[18] Catalysts for the decline are linked to higher prices charged to cover higher excise taxes, increased education regarding the harmful health implications of smoking, mounting restrictions on where people are permitted to smoke, and new ways to help smokers quit. Price increases for cigarettes have more than offset volume declines, leading to revenue gains. However, revenue growth rates have slowed versus prior decades.

Pricing and Mix. Cigarettes' addictive nature makes them a highly price-inelastic product. While price does not affect overall demand, it can impact sales mix. After discount cigarettes gained market share in the early 1990s, Marlboro lowered their price by 20 percent, immediately driving down discounters' market share. Prices fluctuate over time between discount and premium cigarettes and influence the types of cigarettes consumed.

Foreign Markets. For many years, Tobacco firms have sought growth abroad to compensate for contracting domestic demand. For example, around 60 percent of Phillip Morris's revenue is derived overseas, primarily in Europe and Asia.[19]

Positive drivers in overseas markets include high per capita cigarette consumption, rising incomes in developing markets, fewer government restrictions, and a growing preference for American-style cigarettes. According to Universal Corp., one of the world's leading leaf tobacco merchants and processors, the American-style segment of the international market grew at a compound rate of more than 1.4 percent from 1993 to 2003, which is double the rate for overall world cigarette consumption over the same period.

Additionally, according to the World Health Organization, even if overall smoking popularity declined worldwide, population growth and increasing smoking prevalence among women will likely result in an increase in the total number of smokers.

Litigation. The number of claims filed against the US Tobacco industry is staggering. There have been over 4,600 lawsuits. Thus far, the industry has been largely successful in defending itself, and the litigation threat has dissipated slightly versus prior years. The most notable claims came in 1998. Under the Master Settlement Agreement, the tobacco industry was ordered to pay more than $200 billion over a 25-year span to reimburse states for smoking-related health care costs.[20]

Litigation in the Tobacco industry has an interesting side effect: It creates non-barriers to entry. While the largest cigarette manufacturers enjoy economies of scale advantages similar to large Consumer Staples firms in other industries, they also have a disadvantage because of the immense legacy lawsuit charges. These lawsuit damages create an additional cost that smaller, upstart tobacco firms do not have to face (unless there is another round of large-scale lawsuits).

Litigation Globally

In the US, tobacco litigation began in 1954. The first case outside the US wasn't until 1986 in Australia, and the first European case occurred in Finland in 1988. Since then, the number of lawsuits outside the US has gradually risen. In most cases, an individual smoker sues one or more cigarette companies based on an illness he or she claims was caused by smoking. Most individual cases are dismissed.

Source: Philip Morris International.

HOUSEHOLD & PERSONAL PRODUCTS

Non-durable consumer goods are manufactured products that can be divided into two sub-industries: Household Products and Personal Products. Some common items in the Household Products category include cleaning supplies, laundry detergents, garbage bags, paper plates, and cat litter. Virtually all these items can be found at neighborhood supermarkets and comprise approximately 73 percent of the Household & Personal Products industry group.[21]

The other 27 percent is Personal Products, with items generally falling into one of six segments—hair care, cosmetics and fragrances, skin care, deodorants, oral care, and miscellaneous (includes things like shaving products, sunblock, and hair dye).

The global market capitalization of the combined Household & Personal Products industry is around $550 billion and represents about 17 percent of the MSCI World Consumer Staples benchmark.[22] Table 4.9 shows the 10 largest Household & Personal Products (HPP) firms globally, listed by market capitalization.

New HPP products are usually the result of research and development (R&D) efforts. Most firms in this space closely link their R&D departments to marketing. Marketing teams participate in consumer learning initiatives to gain in-depth knowledge of the company's consumers and target markets. Armed with this insight, marketers help decide which new products to roll out and the best ways to design them. While most HPP firms create their packaging designs in-house, many firms purchase containers or packaging from third parties. On average, raw materials used to manufacture products and packaging comprise around 70 percent of the cost of goods sold (COGS). The remaining COGS include labor and factory overhead expenses.

Timeframes in bringing new products to market vary, with some taking several years. Once the product has been designed, it is test marketed to assess commercial viability. If limited distribution tests prove successful, a nationwide rollout follows.

Table 4.9   10 Largest Global Household & Personal Products Companies

Rank	Company	Country	Market Cap (Millions)
1	Procter & Gamble	US	$225,950
2	L'Oréal	France	$88,519
3	Reckitt Benckiser	UK	$41,299
4	Colgate-Palmolive	US	$39,741
5	Kimberly-Clark	US	$29,339
6	Beiersdorf	Germany	$19,526
7	Avon Products	US	$16,961
8	Kao	Japan	$16,525
9	Henkel	Germany	$13,275
10	Shiseido	Japan	$9,707

Source: Thomson Datastream, as of 12/31/2007.

Products are distributed through both wholesale channels and directly to a wide assortment of retailers, including supermarkets, department stores, drugstores, and online merchants. Large supermarket chains, club stores, and Wal-Mart make up the majority of developed market sales. In emerging markets, small retail operators have more influence, where bodegas and other local outlets sell smaller pack sizes appealing to lower-income consumers.

Sales channel mix varies to a degree in the cosmetics business. While many traditional large-format outlets sell cosmetics, other channels include Avon's direct-sales model, which uses independent sales reps to sell products in consumer's homes. Premium, or prestige, cosmetics are sold in specialty cosmetics outlets like Sephora stores, spas and salons, and on television (QVC and infomercials).

Traditional HPP firms like P&G usually sell their products directly to retailers, who usually mark up the products between 25 and 40 percent. Distribution is handled through warehouse systems, where product manufacturers ship end products to regional distribution centers owned and operated by the retail partner. From this point on, the retailer takes over in shipping products to its stores.

Household & Personal Products Drivers The Household & Personal Products industry includes a wide range of items we use every day. We don't "need" these products to survive, like we need food and beverage products, yet we still consider them necessities. The primary drivers of both industries include the following:

> **Brand Equity.** The strongest consumer product companies are able to connect with their customers by building brand equity. Once consumers begin to feel a personal attachment to a product brand, they can often be loyal customers for years. HPP companies compete fiercely through aggressive marketing and packaging ingenuity to build allegiances with consumers. Companies with the strongest brands can command price premiums.

Consumer loyalty accompanying strong brands provides a consistent volume base for consumer products franchises and can also help drive product-line extensions that fuel growth. For example, one of P&G's biggest brands is Tide. You can either buy Tide or any one of 12 Tide extension products (e.g., Ultra Tide Liquid, Tide Powder, Tide to Go). If you don't prefer Original Scent Tide, you can choose from 15 other options. Tide also has separate partner brands such as Downy, Bounce, and Febreze. The original Tide's robust brand equity has fueled over 20 extension products for P&G.

Price. Executives at HPP firms manage pricing carefully. The goal is to take advantage of margin expansion opportunities through premium pricing while not alienating customers. Most manufacturers offer products at a range of different price points to maintain steady overall sales as the economy ebbs and flows.

Fluctuations in consumers' disposable incomes lead to variance in their demand for brand quality. For example, when times are tough, consumers are more likely to "trade down" from a premium-priced brand to a lower priced alternative. The alternative might be a cheaper product manufactured by the same company or a private label good (more on this later) the retailer offers. When times are good, the opposite occurs as more consumers trade up to higher margin, premium-priced products.

Demographics. As with most Consumer Staples industries, demographics play an important role in HPP products. Brand managers study population growth projections and age groups to determine what types of products are most likely to generate mass appeal. For instance, older people tend to be more prevalent consumers of beauty products. Japan's aging population has been a strong demand catalyst for Japanese cosmetic manufacturers like Shiseido and has also lured foreign cosmetics companies to enter the market.

Foreign Markets. Economic growth in developing countries has facilitated rapid increases in consumption of home and personal care products. HPP products that most Americans consider "staples" are just now being discovered by emerging-market citizens with rising disposable incomes. Take toothpaste, for example. Simple table salt is still a common way for people who live in emerging markets to clean their teeth. As more and more people see their incomes rise, they are transitioning to gels, opening high-growth sales channels for international firms selling toothpaste, like Colgate-Palmolive.

Deodorant is another example. Unilever, maker of Axe deodorant, estimates that only 7 out of 100 Asians currently use deodorant, while Russians tend to use it sporadically for special occasions, like weddings.[23] Since there are around 3 billion Asians in the world, Unilever has a major incentive to convince Asians they need to use products like Axe every day.

Innovation. HPP firms are constantly in search of innovations to differentiate their products from peers. Successful innovations add new benefits like convenience and healthfulness to products.

Renowned innovator P&G invests millions of dollars each year in consumer learning research to identify consumers' "unarticulated needs." The company sponsors ethnographic research like "Living It" experiences, where P&G employees fully immerse themselves into consumers' homes to learn what household products could help overcome daily challenges and improve their lives. Based on this research, P&G continually rolls out products that stimulate new demand year after year.

FOOD & STAPLES RETAILERS

So where do you buy all of these Consumer Staples products we've been talking about? You buy them at Food & Staples retailers. The four central sub-industries in the Food & Staples Retailing universe are Hypermarkets & Super centers (44 percent of Food & Staples Retailing), Food Retail (39 percent), Drug Retail (14 percent), and Food Distributors (3 percent).[24]

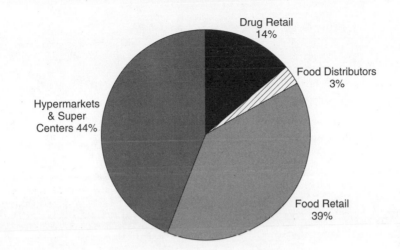

Figure 4.4   Food & Staples Retailing Sub-Industry Composition
Source: Thomson Datastream, as of 12/31/2007.

Figure 4.4 conveys how each sub-industry fits into the Food & Staples Retailing Industry. Since these retailers sell a wide variety of staples products, their businesses are relatively non-cyclical. To give you a feel for a standard Staples retailer's revenue derivation, let's break down how the average American spends $100 on a shopping trip.[25]

- Perishables: $50.10
- Beverages: $8.26
- All other grocery, food: $11.30
- Non-food grocery: $7.94
- Snack foods: $4.42
- Main meal items: $6.84
- Health & beauty care: $3.58
- General merchandise: $4.38
- Pharmacy: $3.18

The global publicly traded Food & Staples Retailing landscape is close to $1 trillion in size and represents about 25 percent of the MSCI World Consumer Staples benchmark.[26] In the US, the number

Table 4.10   Sales by Store Type

Store Type	# of Stores	Annual Sales
Supermarkets	34,967	$535 billion
Drugstores	~24,000	$244 billion
Wholesale Clubs	1,152	$450 billion

Source: Food Marketing Institute, Chain Drug Review.

of stores and annual sales are estimated by store type in Table 4.10. Table 4.11 shows the 10 largest Food & Staples retailers globally. Note Wal-Mart is firmly entrenched as the global leader.

How does this industry operate? Staples retailers source their supply from product manufacturers. Supermarkets and drugstores are traditionally low-margin businesses—both are constantly searching for ways to improve operational efficiency and profitability. In both businesses, the difference between strong and weak operators can be decided by as little as a 1 percent difference in net margins.

Supermarket and drugstore operators are encountering an increasingly competitive environment in recent years because of industry

Table 4.11   Ten Largest Global Food & Staples Retailers

Rank	Company	Country	Market Cap (millions)
1	Wal-Mart Stores	US	$190,348
2	Tesco	UK	$74,471
3	CVS Caremark	US	$58,706
4	Carrefour	France	$54,919
5	Walgreens	US	$37,752
6	Woolworth's	Australia	$36,249
7	Costco Wholesale	US	$30,329
8	Seven & I Holdings	Japan	$28,241
9	Metro	Germany	$27,218
10	Wesfarmers	Australia	$19,374

Source: Thomson Datastream, as of 12/31/2007.

consolidation and maturity. Where there may have been one major grocer per suburban city in the past, competing supermarkets and drugstores are now usually within close proximity to one another.

The rise of supercenters and wholesale clubs further intensified the competitive landscape as companies like Wal-Mart and Costco placed more emphasis on food sales. Wal-Mart has even branched off into filling prescriptions, to the dismay of Walgreens and CVS.

Since wholesale clubs normally win price battles versus traditional supermarkets and drugstores (via economies of scale), the latter have been forced to differentiate their value proposition by creating a more pleasurable, convenient shopping experience. Companies like Safeway and Kroger are increasing capital expenditures on remodeling efforts, creating new store formats offering upgraded displays, full-service bakeries, and a wider range of prepared foods. In many ways, these traditional supermarket operators seem to be moving more toward the Whole Foods model of a top-notch store format that may justify paying a little extra.

Cost control is a preeminent feature of Staples retailers' annual business plans, given how competitive the landscape is. Companies in this space operate on slim margins with even the best-managed retailers paying around 70 to 73 cents in product costs for every dollar of sales. With this type of cost structure, food and drug inflation can significantly impact the bottom line. In order to counteract constantly rising product costs, many retailers have consolidated to increase their purchasing power with suppliers.

Labor costs play a central role in the cost equation, accounting for more than 50 percent of operating expenses for most food retailers. Many supermarket chains are unionized, which creates wage pressure. Also, the supermarket and drugstore industries employ a large percentage of workers at minimum wage, making them sensitive to minimum wage laws. When minimum wage goes up, retailers encounter difficulty passing along labor cost increases to consumers.

Operators in the pharmacy business are finding it increasingly difficult to fill pharmacist job openings due to a shortage of qualified candidates. The National Association of Chain Drug Stores forecasted that the supply of pharmacists would only increase 7.8 percent between

2004 and 2010, while the number of prescriptions dispensed would rise 27 percent. To keep up with the growing number of prescriptions, firms are paying higher salaries and also looking for more ways to automate the prescription-filling process through investments in things like robotics.

Most manufacturers pay Staples retailers slotting fees to get their products on store shelves. The fees subsidize the retailers' upfront costs for adding the product and provide partial protection in case the product does not sell. Other fees retailers commonly charge manufacturers include pay-to-stay fees (payments that guarantee shelf space for existing products), volume incentives, promotions, rebates, free-product discounts, and failure fees (where the manufacturer is obligated to buy back unsold inventory).

While slotting fees can be a benefit to the bottom line, most retailers focus acutely on maintaining inventory most appealing to their customer base. The industry calls this objective *category management*. The intent of category management is to design the merchandise mix most likely to result in profit maximization. Shelf space is planned accordingly, with certain types of products grouped together (e.g., cereals can all be found in the cereal aisle). Category managers are in charge of select business units and work with suppliers to ensure the appropriate sizes and quantities of each product are delivered. But how do category managers know how much of each product to order each month? Point-of-sale (POS) technology is the key.

Point-of-sale equipment installed at cash registers and linked to computer networks read the universal product code labels scanned at checkout counters. The data derived from POS scanners are stored in a database the retailer analyzes on an ongoing basis. Retailers are able to identify optimal sales by size, color, and a host of other factors and make buying decisions accordingly.

Technology is also utilized in the supply chain to speed inventory replenishment. Using "quick response" programs, retailers are electronically linked to their suppliers using a "sell one, send one" approach that facilitates the maintenance of leaner inventories while ensuring adequate merchandise remains on hand to meet consumer demand. These programs are called *electronic data interchanges* (EDI).

Did You Know?

There are, on average, 45,000 items in a typical supermarket. This is why inventory management systems are pivotal in dictating operational efficiency.

Source: Food Marketing Institute.

Wal-Mart—The Behemoth Wal-Mart's impact on the retailing industry has been massive. The firm has become the largest retailer in the world, using its low-price appeal to strip market share from competitors.

What gives Wal-Mart its huge price advantages? To start, Wal-Mart has the most sophisticated technology in retailing. Its computer system is second in size only to the Pentagon.[27] Wal-Mart's computer infrastructure acts as a massive information vault, with the company storing every single cash register receipt for two years.

Wal-Mart also uses technology in unique ways, such as tracking the weather. It does this to capitalize on weather events that normally increase demand for certain products. For instance, Wal-Mart will tell you that when a hurricane is coming, people buy a lot more Pop-Tarts, especially strawberry (yes, their modeling is that precise). So if Wal-Mart thinks a hurricane is likely to head to a particular region, Kellogg is going to receive a big order to ship more strawberry Pop-Tarts.

Wal-Mart has established a unique relationship with its suppliers by making its proprietary data available to them. It set up a retail link allowing suppliers to monitor its inventory in real time. Armed with this data, partners like P&G can optimally manage inventory flows to ensure they have the right product, in the right stores, at the right time. Such an arrangement helps Wal-Mart maintain an efficient mix of inventory while also helping product manufacturers sell more products by positioning them optimally in stores.

Technological efficiency isn't Wal-Mart's only advantage. The company also competes effectively because of its immense scale. Suppliers ship products to one of Wal-Mart's mammoth distribution centers, which efficiently routes the items to stores. Wal-Mart can afford to build huge, automated distribution centers. The net result of these centers is a reduction in per-unit distribution costs. The more products that can travel through one center efficiently, the greater the leverage on the fixed cost investment.

The distribution center in Wal-Mart's hometown of Bentonville, Arkansas, includes 19 1/2 miles of conveyor belts measuring 1.2 million square feet—the size of 24 football fields. There are bar codes on the thousands of cases traveling on conveyor belts in Wal-Mart's 110 distribution centers around the world. Cameras read each bar code and decide which store the package is destined for.[28]

Food & Staples Drivers   Food & Staples retailers share some of the same types of macro drivers as the product manufacturers that supply them. The chief differences arise in retailers' interfacing with end consumers.

> **Demographic Trends.** As the intermediary between product manufacturers and consumers, Staples retailers appeal to a vast array of consumers. Similar to other Consumer Staples industries, the retail end is driven by consumer preferences, which are often driven by demographic trends. For instance, ethnic food has seen increased demand alongside rising immigration. This trend impacts supermarkets, which now devote more shelf space to ethnic foods.
>
> Age is also a big factor, particularly for drugstores. As over 75 million baby boomers age, demand for pharmacy services

---

Shopping Day

Sunday is the most popular day to go grocery shopping—21 percent of Americans head to the supermarket. Saturday is slightly less common at 18 percent, while Friday is the most popular weekday at 14 percent. Who is doing most of the shopping? Sixty-nine percent of the time, it is the female head of household.

Source: Progressive Grocer 72nd Annual Report of the Grocery Industry, April 2005.

and products is poised to steadily grow, since drugs are more often required by elderly people.

Convenience. Convenience is especially pertinent in the pharmacy business since consumers normally desire a quick in-and-out shopping experience. Walgreen Co. and CVS Caremark Corp., the two largest US drugstore operators, normally build their stores in areas that are easily accessible, provide easy parking, and have prominent curb appeal.

Drugstore chains are also offering greater convenience by working with pharmacy benefit managers (PBM), which offer mail-order services. In 2006, prescriptions from mail-order pharmacies grew 10.7 percent to just over $50 billion, commanding a 20 percent market share.[29] In 2007, CVS's acquisition of Caremark was a game changer of sorts in the drug retailing business. Investors and industry executives will be following the combined corporation closely in the coming years to delineate the synergies of combining PBMs with traditional drugstore operators.

To further enhance their value proposition and convenience offering, both Walgreens and CVS have recently acquired convenient care clinics to add to their stores. They are rolling out in-store health clinics staffed with nurse practitioners to target the 30 percent of the population who do not have a primary care physician or the time to visit one. The service is geared toward those suffering from common cold symptoms. CVS, which acquired MinuteClinic in 2006, plans to open around 400 clinics by the end of 2008, eventually adding clinics to 2,500 of its stores.

Convenience is also a factor for supermarket operators. Large supermarket chains like Tesco in the UK and Kroger in the US offer an array of store formats, including smaller convenience stores time-strapped shoppers prefer.

Location. Location is key to supermarket and drugstore success. Retailers carefully analyze regions where they plan new stores, evaluating population growth trends and levels of economic vitality. While real estate is often more expensive in wealthier communities, stores in these areas often benefit from residents with a higher percentage of disposable income, which can lead to greater demand for high margin brands. Competition from other retailers is another facet of the cost-benefit analysis when considering new locations, because levels of store traffic can be influenced accordingly.

Private Label. Private label goods are goods bearing the name of the store. Whole Foods has a higher than average proportion of private label goods, taking advantage of its brand power with consumers to sell its own products. While supermarkets do not typically produce the goods themselves, they realize several benefits by selling them under their own label. First, private label goods carry higher margins to the retailer when compared to average margins on national brands. Second, private label goods can be used to improve the store's image and promote customer loyalty. Third, they are typically offered at a lower price than national brands to consumers (usually anywhere between a 10 to 40 percent discount).

Over the years, private label products have gradually seen increasing acceptance among consumers. While a "trade-down effect" to private labels can be detrimental to the bottom line for product manufacturers, retailers welcome higher sales of private label goods.

Generics. Pharmacies are benefiting from higher sales of generic drugs. Although generics sell at a significant discount to branded drugs (Standard & Poor's estimates costs to be $32.23 for generic versus $111.02 on average for branded), they generate higher gross profits on average—generics have gross margins of at least 50 percent versus branded drugs, which usually have gross margins of around 15 percent. Generics represent about half of the prescriptions filled and are a growing segment, given the exceptionally large number of branded drugs losing patent protection in the next several years.[30]

Chapter Recap

The Consumer Staples sector is comprised of a variety of industries, including Food Products, Beverages, Tobacco, Household Products, Personal Products, and Food & Staples Retailing. While these industries possess similar inelastic demand characteristics, each also possesses unique operating environments and drivers.

- The Food Products industry includes agribusinesses and packaged food companies. Agribusinesses are firms engaged in the middle stages of the food production process, in between the farmer and the final products. Crop processors refine raw commodities into ingredients used in packaged food products. Packaged food producers own the food brands you see on supermarket shelves.

- Drivers of the Food Products industry include population growth, wealth, shifting consumer preferences, demographic shifts, foreign markets, and supply drivers such as weather, competition for resources, and technology advancements.

- The Beverages industry includes Soft Drinks, Brewers, and Distillers & Vintners. Beverages' sub-industries have different operational traits that result in varying profit margins, usually determined by how capital intensive each business is.

- Drivers of the Beverages industry are similar to the Food Products industry and include population growth, wealth, innovation, shifting consumer preferences, distribution, demographics, foreign markets, and consolidation.

- The Tobacco industry is concentrated and dominated by cigarette manufacturing. Tobacco farmers sell tobacco leaves to dealers, who process the tobacco and turn it over to manufacturers, who create finished products.

- Drivers of the Tobacco industry include pricing, mix, foreign markets, and litigation.

- Household Products and Personal Products are nondurable consumer goods that are commonly found in kitchens or bathroom cabinets. Firms operating in these industries spend a lot on R&D in the form of consumer learning to develop new products, which they often manufacture themselves.

- Drivers of the Household Products and Personal Products industries include brand equity, pricing, demographics, foreign markets, and innovation.

- Food & Staples Retailing is made up of food retail (e.g., supermarkets), drug retail (e.g., pharmacies), and hypermarkets and supercenters (e.g., Wal-Mart). These retailers share a common feature—they sell predominantly Consumer Staples items, making their businesses relatively noncyclical.

- Drivers of the Food & Staples Retailing industry include demographics, convenience, location, private labels, and generic drugs.

CHALLENGES IN THE CONSUMER STAPLES SECTOR

Each sector of the stock market faces unique business hurdles. This chapter explores two primary challenges in the Consumer Staples sector:

1. Finding ways to grow in mature industries.
2. Dealing with volatile input costs.

These two challenges apply to opposite ends of the income statement—one impacts revenue while the other impacts earnings. A firm can pursue top-line revenue growth either organically or through acquisition, while bottom-line performance is largely influenced by how firms manage their cost structures.

CHALLENGE 1: GROWING IN MATURE INDUSTRIES

The Consumer Staples sector generally embodies mature industries in developed markets around the world, frequently making growth a challenging endeavor. The primary question facing consumer product firms today: How will the firm generate increasing, repeatable sales from nondurable goods?

Consumer Staples firms seek recurring revenue because it can lead to predictability and consistency in their income statements. Brand allegiance is one vehicle that breeds recurring revenue streams because consumers tend to be fairly loyal (i.e., "sticky") once they adopt a chosen brand, whether it's soda, beer, shampoo, detergent, or ice cream.

Customer stickiness is obviously beneficial in generating repeatable sales, but what about *increasing* top-line sales and market share? Stickiness works against you here, because increasing market share means luring and converting new customers from competing brands, who also have sticky customers. The two primary ways Consumer Staples firms expand market share are through innovation and acquisitions.

Innovation

Innovation is one effective vehicle for organic growth. The most successful innovators are generally unconstrained by conventional wisdom and act as game-changers in their industries. They take measured risks by doing things others haven't yet done; and, if successful, they may alter the competitive landscape by introducing superior products or processes, raising the bar for competitors.

> *"Innovation distinguishes between a leader and a follower."*
> —Steve Jobs, Co-Founder and CEO of Apple, Inc.

The innovator's reward can be a period of excess revenues and profits. Brand stickiness may take hold and prevent defection until competitors can actually *surpass* the first mover's unique value proposition. In other words, simply matching the new idea may not be enough to make any meaningful gains—competitors must build *better* products or otherwise present a more compelling value proposition.

Innovation as an important strategic attribute to Consumer Staples firms might seem a bit counterintuitive. Though the general Consumer Staples product types generally don't change rapidly, there are continually new variances or incremental improvements. To remain competitive, Staples firms must identify new functional benefits that might entice new customers and seize market share.

The primary differentiating feature of Consumer Staples innovation from other industries is the intense consumer focus. Much of the R&D budget for a consumer goods firm is spent on consumer learning research outside of labs. Staples firms spend millions every year building insights on what drives consumer buying decisions. Types of consumer learning include:

- Focus groups
- Customer satisfaction surveys
- Brand awareness tracking
- Segmentation studies
- Quantitative market analysis
- Ethnographic research
- And others

Innovation in Practice—Procter & Gamble

A widely known example of a consumer firm with a culture based on innovation is Procter & Gamble. Innovation is promoted at P&G by the firm's marketing and R&D expenditures, which remain consistent as a percentage of revenue year to year, independent of the macroeconomic backdrop. Procter & Gamble currently invests more than $200 million a year in consumer research geared toward understanding both the articulated and unarticulated needs of consumers. Articulated needs are self-explanatory. Unarticulated needs are the things consumers don't tell you in focus groups but show you based on behavior.

One example of innovation: P&G consumer research unveiled that, while half the population desired whiter teeth, only one-tenth took action—paying a dentist several hundred dollars to do it. Procter & Gamble recognized this opportunity and developed a delivery method for a peroxide gel that could be easily applied to teeth and removed within 30 minutes. This was introduced to consumers as Crest Whitestrips.

(Continued)

Organic growth through innovation doesn't always involve totally new products. It can also stem from incremental improvements to existing product lines. Another P&G example is Febreze. Originally launched in 1998 to strip odor from fabrics, by 2001 it had about half the market share in the $300 million global market for fabric refreshers. It appeared there wasn't much room left to grow.

Procter & Gamble surveyed consumers and found most were happy with the scent, but they used it rather infrequently. Procter & Gamble's conclusion: To grow the brand, the product should be repositioned in a way calling for more frequent use. In 2004, P&G unleashed Febreze's scent into air freshener sprays, scented candles, and even added its scent to other P&G brands like Tide and Bounce. The incremental innovation has more than doubled Febreze's annual sales, making it a $750 million brand.

Source: AG Lafley and Ram Charan, *The Game Changer: How You Can Drive Revenue and Profit Growth with Innovation,* (Crown Business: 2008), 96.

Evaluating Innovation as an Investor   Unfortunately, forecasting innovation is akin to making a blind weather forecast. Consumer goods firms regularly talk up innovation on their quarterly conference calls. But if a firm is talking about an early stage product on a conference call, it's likely not a breakthrough idea. Consumer Staples firms generally prefer not to show their hands with regard to a big innovation by saying, "Hey competition, we have a big idea we are rolling out next year. Here it is—now go copy it."

As an investor, your first goal with regard to assessing innovation should be to ignore speculative innovation hoopla because it's likely an unreliable indicator. Reality is only about one idea out of 1,000 generates over $100 million in sales—the barometer of success for the biggest consumer packaged goods firms.

Consumer goods industry innovation is all about commercialization and execution. If a firm can do those two things well, it should find innovation success more consistently than its peers. In the process, that can lead to getting the shelving, pricing, and merchandising it's after and building brand awareness with consumers.

Growth via Acquisition

There's an alternative to organic growth if the innovation well runs dry—you can always buy someone else's innovation! Mergers and acquisitions (M&A) have long been a common growth strategy for Consumer Staples firms because the synergy opportunities are very real.

Consumer packaged goods firms find synergies in procurement when it comes to buying things like plastics, which are often used in packaging. They also find synergies when their combined operations lead to enhanced leverage with retailers and advertising media buying. Distribution synergies often allow an acquirer to immediately give a smaller brand a shot in the arm—simply putting the product on its trucks and introducing the item to its retail partners. Synergies are also easy to produce in back-office operations like billing, which is standardized in the consumer goods industry. These types of synergies are often key ingredients behind successful M&A deals.

Good deals are generally quickly margin accretive and allow firms to simply buy their way into higher margin businesses. Procter & Gamble didn't get to $200 billion in market capitalization on innovation alone. They've also made a number of acquisitions through the years, penetrating higher margin categories like cosmetics, health care products, and even pet care (with Iams pet food).

M&A Trends

Mergers and acquisitions activity in the Consumer Staples sector goes through peaks and valleys. Deal frequency hit a particularly fevered pitch toward the end of the 1990s and again in 2005 and 2006, as shown in Figure 5.1. There is a cascading effect when merger mania heats up. As competitors do deals to increase their scale advantages and market shares, executives at peer companies feel pressure to defend their turf and also engage in acquisitions. It pays to follow M&A trends because when deals accelerate in the sector you can start keeping an eye out for the next logical takeover candidates.

(Continued)

Buying a takeover target prior to a deal is one of the best ways to achieve outsized short-term returns in the Consumer Staples sector.

Unfortunately, it's not as easy as it may seem. Often, firms that seem like obvious takeover targets get bid up to rich valuations in expectation of a deal. If a deal doesn't emerge, those rich valuations can weigh on the long-term performance of that firm's shares. Unless you have some special skill identifying takeover targets, focusing on firms with strong attributes and solid long-term prospects is usually the best bet.

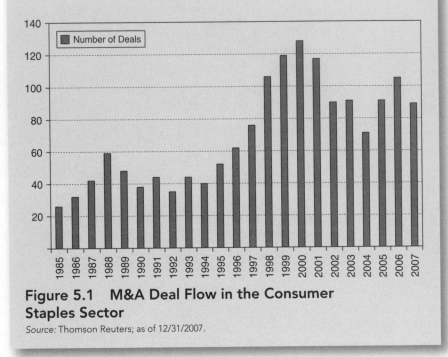

Figure 5.1   M&A Deal Flow in the Consumer Staples Sector
Source: Thomson Reuters; as of 12/31/2007.

Analyzing M&A   How does M&A impact the sector? It depends on how deals are transacted. When one firm acquires another by paying cash (either with cash on hand or with borrowed funds), the acquired firm ceases to exist as an independent, publicly traded firm. Those shares are removed from the market and sector share supply declines. Because stock prices are dictated by supply and demand, this should have a positive impact on prices if the demand for Consumer Staples shares remains constant or rises. This bullish force becomes more powerful if the sector as a whole experiences a high level of cash-based mergers.

But mergers can also be transacted in stock. For example, Firm A is worth $20 billion and Firm B is worth $10 billion—$30 billion in total stock supply. Say Firm A wants to buy B. Usually they'll pay a premium, maybe 20 percent—paying $12 billion. Firm A issues $12 billion in new Firm A stock, and B ceases to exist. Where we once had $30 billion in total stock supply, we now have $32 billion. If this happens broadly, this can have a negative impact on prices sector-wide if demand for Consumer Staples shares doesn't keep pace.

Deals can also be transacted partially in cash, partially in stock. For example, Firm A might pay a hybrid of $6 billion in cash, $6 billion in stock for B. But most cash/stock deals tend to result in lower overall supply, which can be a bullish factor.

How do you know when cash-based deals or cash/stock hybrid deals are more likely to occur? Watch bond yields and earnings yields. A bond yield represents a firm's borrowing cost. The earnings yield is the reverse of the P/E ratio—the E/P (earnings per share over price per share). When earnings yields are higher than bond yields, a firm can borrow cheaply and buy a higher earnings yield—the difference between the higher earnings yield and the lower bond yield is profit. Done right, the deal finances itself and is immediately accretive to the acquirer's earnings. The acquirer's earnings per share rises, and, all else being equal, share price should follow. This is powerful incentive for CEOs to transact acquisitions (or buy back their own shares—the same concepts apply). Periods likely to see a higher rate of mergers and acquisitions are when interest rates are generally benign and bond yields are lower than earnings yields—just as we saw in 2005, 2006, and 2007.

That's the sector-wide impact, but the effect on individual stocks can be subject to other considerations entirely, at least in the short term. In the very near term, sometimes Wall Street reacts favorably to deal news, sometimes negatively. As an investor, it's critical you don't get swayed by near-term knee-jerk reactions and understand how a deal impacts a firm for the longer term. For a deal to work, firms should find targets that fit well into their existing business or somehow introduce a new, competitive value proposition.

Acquisition Gone Right—Quaker Oats/Gatorade   But what happens after the marriage? Quaker Oats provides some good examples of acquisition gone right and an acquisition gone wrong. Quaker Oats, founded in 1891, started in ready-to-eat cereal, but it quickly diversified, buying businesses throughout the twentieth century. Arguably, its most important acquisition was Gatorade in 1983. When Quaker bought Gatorade's owner Stokely-Van Camp, Inc. for $220 million, consensus was that it overpaid. The year before, Gatorade generated only $90 million in sales (0.1 percent of the domestic beverage market at that time). A food analyst said, "To get in a bidding war for a mediocre company like Stokely is ridiculous."[1] However, Gatorade had a 97 percent share of the sports drink market. This dominant share, in a category capable of substantial growth, enticed Quaker. After selling off nearly all of Stokely's business lines, the net acquisition price was $95 million.

By 1989, Gatorade generated $125 million annual profits (one-fifth Quaker's overall). *BusinessWeek* called the acquisition one of the 1980s' best. Then, in 2000, Pepsi bought Quaker Oats for $13.4 billion in stock, thereby acquiring the preeminent non-carbonated drink brand.[2]

Gatorade's Famous Fans

A lot of Gatorade's success can be attributed to luck.

Without any urging by Stokely's marketing teams, the drink became a favorite of Elvis Presley. During his performances in the late 1960s and early 1970s, he would talk to fans about things he was into, like karate. Frequently, he'd also mention Gatorade. "They give this stuff to athletes," he said. "It's supposed to work 12 times faster than water."

Another serendipitous marketing gift came in 1985 when New York Giants nose guard Jim Burt spontaneously grabbed a Gatorade cooler after a victory over the Redskins and dumped it on coach Bill Parcells as time expired. Parcells took it well—really well. He was superstitious and allowed his players to continue dunking him into the 1986 season. The Giants went 14–2 that season, winning the Superbowl. Gatorade dunks have become a ritual ever since (although most teams use water these days—Parcells ruined most of his game-day clothes after getting doused with more than 80 gallons of Gatorade that season).

Source: Darren Rovell, *First in Thirst: How Gatorade Turned the Science of Sweat Into a Cultural Phenomenon,* (AMACOM Books, 2006), 57.

Quaker Oats ran a textbook brand-building campaign after acquiring Gatorade in 1983. From 1984 to 1990, Quaker ran television ads using a successful jingle that said it all: "Gatorade is thirst aid, for that deep down body thirst!" The jingle caught on so well that, in 1987, an advertising survey demonstrated that 79.2 percent of consumers could fill the phrase: "_____ is thirst aid" with the word "Gatorade." Sales rose under the "Thirst Aid" campaign by 25 percent a year through 1990, approaching $900 million annually.[3]

Up until 1990, Gatorade largely relied on natural sporting events to help build its image. The executives at Stokely had aimed not to create any staged imaging, fearing the brand might lose some of its legitimacy. By 1990, however, sports marketing was changing. Athletes were signing on to endorse products like beverages with increasing frequency. For example, basketball star Magic Johnson promoted Pepsi, while Michael Jordan had a contract with Coke.

Jordan was a natural spokesman for Gatorade because he played in Quaker's hometown of Chicago. Quaker signed the Chicago Bulls star in 1990 right after his contract with Coke expired. "Be Like Mike" was the first major ad campaign using Michael Jordan to promote Gatorade. The ads were a huge hit. The new message: Kids everywhere could be like their hero just by drinking Gatorade.

As Jordan's Chicago Bulls won title after title in the early 1990s, his appeal as a spokesman grew in stature, helping Gatorade's distribution potential. Quaker was able to use his visibility overseas to help launch international sales of Gatorade to 26 new markets. Jordan also helped Quaker gain leverage with supermarkets and premium shelf space with Wal-Mart. For the first time, Gatorade passed oatmeal in sales at Quaker.

The primary factor making Gatorade a successful acquisition for Quaker was maintaining a consistent brand image for Gatorade as the preferred drink of professional athletes—a quality not easily duplicated by competitors. Quaker established the Gatorade Sports Science Institute in Barrington, Illinois, as a testament the company was committed to staying on the cutting edge of performance-enhancement beverages. Shrewd marketing, small incremental changes to the product's design, and a little luck helped Gatorade maintain 80 percent market share and increase sales tenfold in 10 years, from $100 million to $1 billion.

Acquisition Gone Bad: Quaker Oats/Snapple Buoyed by the success of the Gatorade venture from the 1980s, Quaker Oats added another non-carbonated beverage brand to its arsenal in the 1990s by purchasing Snapple for $1.7 billion in 1994. At the time of purchase, it was a hot upstart in the increasingly popular ready-to-drink (RTD) tea category. By 1997, however, the Snapple acquisition would result in over $1 billion in losses for Quaker, be mentioned in deal circles as one of the decades' worst acquisitions, cost both the chairman and the president of Quaker their jobs, and ultimately contributed to the end of Quaker's independent existence (it was acquired several years later by Pepsi).

Snapple was created in 1972 under the name Unadulterated Food Products, Inc., by two window-washing brothers-in-law and a health food store owner. The founders distributed fruit juices and all-natural sodas to health stores in New York City and entered the iced tea market in 1987. They used amateurish package designs and adopted the slogan, "Made from the best stuff on earth." As sales mounted, the Thomas H. Lee Company of Boston took an interest, completing a leveraged buyout of the company in 1992. The firm renamed the brand "Snapple" and took it public a year later.[4]

Snapple maintained its offbeat image after becoming a public company. The company rolled out a memorable marketing campaign using one of their employees who had a thick New York accent, Wendy Kaufman, as the "face" of Snapple.

Snapple distribution channels were also unique at the time. It didn't have the capital to propel a national supermarket rollout, so it concentrated its efforts on the so-called "cold channel"—employing small distributors who served thousands of lunch counters and delis selling single-serve refrigerated beverages. The distribution force started small, but emerged as a marketing juggernaut over time. By 1994, Snapple was being sold across the country. Distributors had expanded from the cold channel and acquired a presence in supermarkets, ballooning Snapple's sales from just $4 million to $674 million in 10 years.[5]

Snapple had captured meaningful market share by being an early mover in the RTD tea category. The company was viewed as innovative after pioneering the hot packaged process for teas and developing novel glass-front vending machines to display its bottles. But by 1994, Snapple was challenged by new entrants flooding the market (Arizona Iced Teas, Nantucket Nectars, and Mystic joined Nestea—a Coke joint venture—and Lipton—a Pepsi joint venture—in carving away market share from Snapple). The company lost half its market value from 1993 to 1994. Change was necessary to compete and continue growing.

Snapple's success as an innovator attracted the attention of Quaker Oats, who viewed Snapple as a natural pairing with its Gatorade brand. Quaker had the capital to compete more effectively with Coke and Pepsi and saw an opportunity for both national and international expansion with Snapple, as well as an opportunity to create economy of scale synergies. Quaker bought Snapple in December of 1994 for $1.7 billion.[6]

Quaker's goal after the acquisition was to rationalize distribution and promote synergies. Specifically, Quaker sought to use Snapple's strength in cold-channel (delis) distribution to benefit Gatorade, while using Gatorade's strength in the warm channel (supermarkets) to facilitate growth for Snapple. Quaker attempted to persuade distributors to cede the supermarket accounts they had acquired for Snapple for rights to distribute Gatorade to their cold-channel accounts. Distributors resisted, countering that Snapple's margins were double what they could make on Gatorade. Distributors concluded Quaker was trying to wrestle away hard-earned supermarket accounts without offering a valuable enough consolation prize.[7] Distribution rationalization never occurred.

Quaker also fumbled in packaging. It had successfully introduced Gatorade in a variety of sizes, but consumers didn't like Snapple delivered in 32- and 64-ounce bottles. Gatorade worked because in many instances people drank it following exercise, when they were especially thirsty and in need of rehydration. But Snapple's core function was as a lunchtime beverage, where a 16-ounce bottle was ideal.

The missteps kept coming. Quaker thought it could improve Snapple's image by rolling out more professional commercials and parting ways with Wendy—and Snapple lost a piece of its character. Snapple also parted ways with two radio personalities that had been endorsers—Rush Limbaugh and "shock jock" Howard Stern. Limbaugh went away relatively peacefully, but Stern took issue with the company, engaging in long, on-air diatribes urging his listeners to stay away from "Crapple."[8]

Snapple's sales declined each year after peaking in 1994, the year Quaker bought the company. By 1997, Quaker was in active negotiations to sell, but only Nelson Peltz's Triarc Companies, Inc., was willing to do a deal. Triarc bought Snapple for around $300 million, resulting in over a $1 billion loss for Quaker.

The greatest irony: Three short years later, in 2000, Triarc sold Snapple Beverage Group to Cadbury Schweppes for $1.45 billion.[9] It seemed the problem wasn't that Snapple had passed its prime. It was that Quaker didn't foresee a fundamental cultural mismatch between themselves and Snapple. They tried to duplicate their Gatorade success, but Snapple required a different style of brand management. Triarc's culture was more commensurate with Snapple's—they won back most of Snapple's former distributors. Triarc brought a playful nature back to the brand's marketing and soon had a successful turnaround trophy to put on its wall.

An M&A Framework   Analyzing M&A at the individual stock level is difficult because every deal has different dimensions. To increase your success, you need a systematic framework for analyzing deals. A good framework for Consumer Staples firms includes the following steps:

Step 1: Identify and assess the synergy prospects. Are there real synergies? How long will they take to filter through to the bottom line?

Step 2: Analyze the qualitative aspects to the deal. Will the acquirer be able to effectively manage the newly acquired brand based on its track record? Are there integration risks like in the conflict between Snapple's distribution agents and Quaker?

Step 3: Examine the quantitative aspects to the deal. Compare the price tag of the acquisition to similar deals of recent past, using fundamental valuation analysis techniques. For instance, was the target's Enterprise Value/EBITDA ratio high or low compared to similar deals? What does the firm's Return on Equity look like compared to other firms who were taken over? Ultimately, you want to know: Are the multiples paid by the acquirer justified or not, based on this type of analysis? Often, the market will answer this question by how it initially reacts to the deal news. That said, you're still well served to conduct your own independent analysis.

M&A Kryptonite—Monopoly Status

The best areas to find Consumer Staples takeover targets are places where there are not as many anti-trust concerns. For instance, in the fragmented beer industry, InBev and Anheuser-Busch came to terms in 2008 on a $60 billion transaction. Kings of the fragmented confectionary business, Wrigley and Mars, also came to terms and decided to merge in the same year.

For comparison, ask yourself if P&G would ever buy Colgate. Probably not, because they'd have a near monopoly in the dental market with Crest and Colgate combined. A deal like that would likely see a lot of pushback from regulators.

CHALLENGE 2: DEALING WITH VOLATILE INPUT COSTS

"Trimming the fat" equates to cutting costs in the consumer packaged goods world, and it's a challenge with no end. If AG Lafley were to remain P&G's CEO for the next 32 years, he likely would still enter his office each morning with a goal of trimming fat from P&G.

Fact: As businesses grow, inefficiencies are continually born. Executive teams within consumer products firms are constantly aiming to make their organizations run with more precision. They study cost structure, continually searching for ways to optimize operations. The barometer of success relative to these efforts is profit margins. The

"I hate to say it but this is my 32nd year and there's still fat to trim, okay? It's not because we don't work at it; it's not because we don't have 138,000 P&Gers working their hardest every day around the world. It's simply because there are always ways to do things more simply, and that's what we're focused on. We are focused on simplicity and productivity."

—AG Lafley, Procter & Gamble's CEO, during the company's Q4 2008 quarterly conference call most efficiently run firms normally generate the best margins in their peer group, resulting in higher profits, more favorable treatment from Wall Street, and maximization of shareholder value.

Input Cost Challenges

The Consumer Staples sector as a whole is generally price inelastic, but that doesn't mean pricing isn't a factor in determining winners and losers within the sector. Generally speaking, lower cost producers have pricing advantages, which improve their value proposition. Consumers may not let price influence *whether* they buy a type of Consumer Staples good, but they do consider price when determining *which* brand they buy. In this way, cost control's effect on pricing ability acts as a driver for top-line revenue growth. Wal-Mart is a great example. Wal-Mart generates more revenues than any other retailer, predicated on its superior management of costs, which facilitates its "Every Day Low Price" model.

More important than its influence on the top line, however, is how cost structure impacts the bottom line. When a Staples firm starts to see rising prices on key raw materials used in product manufacturing, margin pressure is likely to soon follow.

Application Hypothetically, if Firm X's cost of goods sold (COGS—an income statement line item showing direct costs attributable to the production of goods, like raw materials and direct labor costs) on Brand Z soap is $5 and they sell the final product to the consumer for $10, they have a 50 percent gross margin on the product. Here's how you would run the calculation:

$$\text{Gross Margin \%} = \frac{\text{Revenue} - \text{Cost of Goods Sold}}{\text{Revenue}}$$

$$\text{Gross Margin \%} = \frac{\$10 - \$5}{\$10}$$

$$= \frac{\$5}{\$10}$$

$$= 50\%$$

If input costs rise 10 percent, COGS goes up by $0.50 to $5.50. If Firm X has a lot of pricing power with Brand Z soap and raises prices by the full $0.50 cost increase (unlikely in most cases), revenue per package of soap climbs to $10.50. In this optimistic scenario, here's what happens to gross margins:

$$\text{Gross Margin \%} = \frac{\$10.50 - \$5.50}{\$10.50}$$
$$= \frac{\$5}{\$10.50}$$
$$= 47.6\%$$

Even though Firm X raised its price in exact proportion to its cost increase, it still saw gross margins fall 2.4 percent. That's just how the math works out and is normal in periods of rising raw material costs.

Firms operating in the same industries normally have similar input costs filtering through the COGS line of their income statement, and all are impacted by periods of rising commodity costs. For instance, if oil prices go up, both Colgate-Palmolive and Kimberly-Clark will be paying more to package (plastics used in packaging are a derivative of oil) and ship their products. If corn prices go up, both Kellogg and General Mills will see their input costs increase related to the production of cereal and other food products. All this leads to one important takeaway: Commodities matter in the Consumer Staples sector.

There are several common ways Staples firms attempt to deal with input cost challenges.

- Hedging
- Pricing
- Changing product formulations
- Restructuring

Hedging To hedge against rising input costs, a consumer products manufacturer might consider buying forward or futures contracts on commodities that are key inputs. A *forward contract* is a private trading agreement between two parties betting on opposite sides of commodity price direction over a certain period. A *futures contract* is the same type of contractual agreement to buy or sell a commodity or financial instrument at a pre-determined price, but the contracts are traded under stricter standards on an exchange. Forward and futures bets allow consumer products firms to hedge commodity risk. If they are long a commodity that spikes in price, the favorable return helps offset the adverse effect on their business operations from the rising input costs.

Who has an incentive to sell the contract to the consumer products firm? Either speculators, who are betting against a particular commodity to make a profit, or business owners, who like the consumer products firm just want to mitigate some of their business risk. Corn farmers might sell a futures contract to protect their bottom line should corn prices tumble due to oversupply.

Hedging is a valuable tool that can help shield net earnings from gross margin erosion. The tricky part for investors lies in the fact that hedging can work for or against firms to different degrees, depending on how successful they are in their trading methods.

Pricing   Most Consumer Staples categories exhibit low price elasticity, allowing firms to pass along cost increases to consumers. However, implementation lag between rising costs and price increases often leads to temporary margin pressure, making it difficult for firms to keep pace on a quarterly basis. Also, to ensure they don't deviate too much from the pack and possibly lead to loss of market share, firms carefully monitor their competitors' pricing strategies.

Product Formulations   Some consumer goods manufacturers have the ability to reformulate their products, using less expensive alternate inputs. P&G, for instance, has spent years redesigning its products, using a variety of different types of raw materials and testing consumer appeal through focus groups. Through these upfront efforts, P&G can mitigate cost pressure through reformulating select products when it encounters periods when certain commodities are rising faster than others. The company uses computer modeling to help forecast whether consumers are likely to accept redesigned products as comparable in quality.[10]

Restructuring While gross margins are usually at the mercy of input costs and pricing, operating margins can be more easily driven by management. The difference between gross margins and operating margins lies in what happens with Selling, General & Administrative (SG&A) expenses. SG&A refers to direct and indirect selling expenses (e.g., advertising), as well as general and administrative expenses associated with business operations (e.g., electricity bills, salaries of non-sales personnel). During periods of rising input costs, firms focus on margin pressure by improving supply chain efficiency and restructuring operations, which can reduce SG&A expenses and enhance operating margins. This offsets some of the raw material pressure felt on the COGS line of an income statement. Common tactics to increase efficiency include improving distribution logistics and utilizing technology to better manage the manufacturing and inventory process.

Improving logistics involves anything that helps reduce per-unit distribution costs. An example of a responsive logistics maneuver during a period of high oil prices would be reducing transportation costs by closing manufacturing facilities and centralizing manufacturing closer to end customers.

An example of technology driving efficiency gains is just-in-time (JIT) inventory. This strategy "trims fat" because firms receive goods only as they're needed, reducing excess inventory and improving returns on capital. To utilize JIT, firms must be proficient at accurately forecasting demand, which usually involves computer modeling. JIT is a departure from the older inventory model of "just-in-case," where firms carried larger-than-necessary inventories to stay ready to meet any level of demand. Just-in-time helps generate savings for retailers by reducing working capital requirements and smooth out order flow for consumer product manufacturing partners.

Challenged by Input Costs: Pilgrim's Pride To illustrate how input costs can pose significant challenges for individual companies, we will examine the largest chicken producer in the US: Pilgrim's Pride. During 2007 and 2008, Pilgrim's top two input costs, corn and soybeans (for chicken feed), shot up in price. Pilgrim's reported grain costs had jumped 41 percent from the previous year. Meanwhile, chicken was priced around $1.34 a pound, below the five-year average of $1.63 a pound. Pilgrim's faced significant hurdles but failed to meaningfully deploy any input cost strategies.

Hedging. Pilgrim's didn't use hedging to balance its input cost risk when these grains were rising in the first half of 2008. So when corn and soybean prices increased, they directly detracted from margins. In the second half of the year, the firm did attempt aggressive hedging tactics to capitalize on what it thought would be a continued surge in grain prices. Unfortunately for Pilgrim's, they bet the wrong way by going long just when commodity prices started plunging. This development exacerbated their operational problems and contributed to very poor financial results late in the year.

Pricing. Pilgrim's also had very little pricing power. Like all commodities, chicken prices are supply-and-demand driven. Yearly demand for chicken is fairly steady, so price swings are usually supply driven. Chicken (also known as broilers) is also a commoditized good—fully fungible—with very little brand power to justify above-average pricing. It so happened that chicken was plentiful between the summers of 2007 and 2008, leading to flat pricing and creating a commodity-driven perfect storm. Figure 5.2 shows how Pilgrim's input squeeze came about. The graph indexes corn, soybeans, and broilers to 100 (as of August 2007) to illustrate comparative price performance of the three commodities over the course of the next year.

Because the firm lacked pricing power (evident by the flat line in broiler prices), the bottom line was held hostage by its main input costs—corn and soybeans.

Given the firm's sensitivity to input costs, Pilgrim's stock traded at a very high negative correlation to corn prices—its

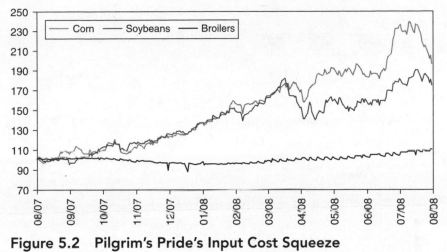

Figure 5.2   Pilgrim's Pride's Input Cost Squeeze

Source: Thomson Datastream.

top input cost. As seen in Figure 5.3, Pilgrim's stock traded in the opposite direction of corn most of the time. As corn rose, Pilgrim's stock fell, running a –0.86 rolling correlation to corn and an R^2 of .74 (R^2 = the correlation squared). This implies that 74 percent of the variance in Pilgrim's stock was related to corn price movement.

Product Reformulations. Pilgrim's wasn't able to do much reformulation to offset input cost pressure. Chicken feed consists

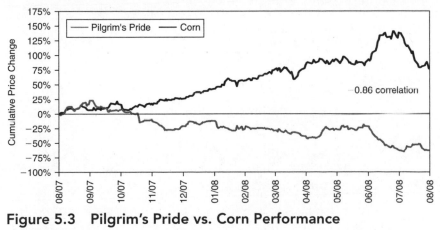

Figure 5.3   Pilgrim's Pride vs. Corn Performance

Source: Thomson Datastream.

of agricultural commodities like corn and soybeans, allowing little room for product reformulations.

Restructuring. As is customary for firms dealing with high raw material pressure, Pilgrim's began to take steps to reduce SG&A expenses through restructuring. By August 2008, the firm closed three chicken processing plants, seven distribution centers, and cut over 2,000 jobs.[11]

While these restructuring efforts will cut costs and pay dividends down the road, as of this writing, Pilgrim's business will not fundamentally improve until either corn prices fall, chicken prices rise, or they find a new way to offset input cost pressure.

Homework—Following Commodity Trends　Part of your regular homework as a Consumer Staples investor is staying abreast of what's happening in the commodity markets. Specifically, you should attempt to identify which commodities play the most central role in the cost structure of companies you own and then track those commodities periodically. You can find quotes for commodities in the *Wall Street Journal* or virtually anywhere else you could regularly check stock quotes. Bloomberg is one source where you can obtain an aggregate snapshot of the basic commodities (http://www.bloomberg.com/markets/commodities/cfutures.html).

Chapter Recap

Consumer goods firms face a host of challenges. Two of the foremost challenges for firms in the Consumer Staples sector include finding ways to generate growth in mature industries and dealing with volatile input costs. Firms grow organically via innovation and inorganically through acquisitions. Input costs fluctuate in sympathy with commodity markets. Companies attempt to deal with input cost strains in a variety of ways, including through hedging, pricing, product reformulations, and restructuring.

Innovation is "playing offense" in the business world and is a primary lever of organic growth and market share expansion.

- Firms that enjoy innovation success are consistent in their R&D quarter-to-quarter expenses. There is no great way to forecast future innovation success other than relying on past management performance and reputation. Buy innovation champions when you can get them at a cheap price.
- Mergers and acquisitions are commonplace in the Consumer Staples sector. The best deals involve targets that are consistent with current operations from a brand fit perspective, come at a fair price, offer myriad synergy opportunities, and are margin accretive early on.
- Pricing is ultra-competitive in the consumer products world, making firms sensitive to rising input costs.
- Firms hedge input costs by buying forward or futures contracts, taking price increases, reformulating products using alternate inputs, and restructuring to reduce SG&A expenses.
- Part of your regular homework as a Consumer Staples investor is to follow the price movements of commodities.

CONSUMER STAPLES IN EMERGING MARKETS

Renowned management consultant Peter Drucker emphasized the study of demographic trends—he called them the future that has already happened.

And in few places are demographic trends more powerful or pertinent today than in emerging markets (EM) for the Consumer Staples sector. While the sector generally consists of mature industries in the developed world, product penetration rates of core Consumer Staples items are much lower in emerging markets, opening potential market opportunities for firms with international distribution platforms.

OPPORTUNITY KNOCKS

In 2005, the developed world represented just 15 percent of the global population yet was a dominant 79 percent of the global economy. At the same time, EM represented 85 percent of the global population and a mere 21 percent of the global economy.[1]

The contrast likely won't last forever. As it fades, powerful growth opportunities will continually materialize in the undeveloped world.

Emerging market countries are making gains on the developed world as more and more of their approximately five billion people join the burgeoning middle class.

What Is Middle Class?

What constitutes as middle class in emerging markets can differ from the developed world's definition. Goldman Sachs defines the "world" middle-class range (inclusive of developed and undeveloped countries) as those earning between $6,000 and $30,000 per year in purchasing-power-parity terms.

Technology and communication advances over the last 20 years have made for an increasingly global landscape for corporations, enabling them to open manufacturing and distribution facilities around the world and spread business and intellectual capital to regions that previously lacked much of either. The benefits include accelerated job creation, higher standards of living in many of the poorest parts of the world, and the creation of a massive new segment of consumers for multinational corporations (MNCs) to target. An astounding two billion people could join the global middle class by 2030. Should that occur, it would dwarf the nineteenth-century middle-class expansion that accompanied the Industrial Revolution.

As profiled in Chapter 2, past periods of profound economic acceleration generally coincided with many items we now consider "consumer staples" becoming ingrained in daily lives. Recall some of the historical underpinnings that paved the way to the current developed world's consumer economy. Wider availability of credit has long been a central ingredient to an expansion in consumerism—one US example was the 1700s, when credit facilities emerged as trade with Europe expanded. The Industrial Revolution in the 1800s brought large-scale manufacturing and massive job creation. In the 1920s, the US was becoming electrified, enabling new technologies like washing machines and refrigerators. And the 1950s saw the emergence of televisions, which joined radio in providing companies with substantial advertising capabilities.

These events played out separately over the last three centuries in the developed world but are happening nearly *simultaneously* in emerging markets. Stores are offering their customers credit for the first time. Emerging nations are becoming hubs for global manufacturing. Basic electricity infrastructure is making its way into distant villages globally, opening up a vast new spectrum of possibilities the developed world takes for granted. People in the BRIC (Brazil, Russia, India, and China) nations are buying TVs and computers, allowing western firms to advertise to previously unreachable consumers.

The scale of the emerging market opportunity for global consumer packaged good firms is immense. However, there are some caveats. Building market share in EM is no cakewalk—it's becoming a crowded, competitive playing field. This chapter highlights key strategies some firms are using to penetrate these markets and provides context to help you analyze, on a forward-looking basis, how increasing EM operations might impact sector and industry (and even firm) performance.

EMERGING MARKETS AND CONSUMER PRODUCTS

More than four billion people live on less than $2 a day. For many years, large consumer product companies generally assumed this represented a non-viable market. While the individual buying power for those earning less than $2 per day certainly presents challenges, in aggregate there is a significant latent opportunity.

Multinational corporations can create vast new markets if they can solve the puzzle of providing profitable products to emerging markets consumers. The first step is to drop preconceived notions on merchandise product development. Simply stated, EM countries are a different ballgame. This presents complications for MNCs that relied on many of the same growth and execution strategies for years. To be successful in emerging markets, a company must fundamentally alter how they design, manufacture, distribute, and market products.

Matching EM Consumer Needs

Product innovation requires tweaking business plans to meet the highly individualized needs of the typical EM consumer. After years of trial and error and large-scale investment in ethnographic research, here are some innovative approaches MNCs are using to successfully roll out products to the masses.

The first requirement is to cultivate an ability to produce quality products at affordable prices. A rapidly evolving approach to encourage consumption in developing markets is the use of single-serve products. Wealthier people in developed markets take for granted the ability to buy goods in bulk, storing the extras in their pantries or refrigerators. Multinational corporations have learned the world's poor live much more day to day because of their unpredictable (and meager) income streams. They buy goods when they have cash in hand from a day's work, making single-serve packaging ideal for their needs. In the developing world, you can buy single-use packs of shampoo, ketchup, aspirin, and other everyday products.

Single-serve products pose challenges for product manufacturers. For one, brand allegiance is more fragile because switching costs are minimal. If a woman buys a sachet of shampoo and is unhappy with it, she can switch brands the very next day—requiring products to be of high quality, in addition to being inexpensive.

Single-serve also requires firms to adopt a different fundamental business model than the one used in the developed world. The basic economics of emerging markets are predicated on small-unit packages, low profit margin per unit, high volume, and high return on capital. Return on capital measures how effectively a firm uses funds invested in its operations. You can have high return on capital despite low profit margin per unit, if you don't need to invest a lot of capital to generate the profit. This model differs from the developed world, where the model is large-unit packs, high margin per unit (in relation to EM), high volume, and reasonable return on capital.[2]

Let's run through a simplified example of how the EM business model works.

Application

Company A and Company B are consumer packaged good manufacturers of shampoo. Company A incorporates a business model representative of the developed world and produces large bottles of shampoo, while Company B employs the single-serve, EM business model. Table 6.1 shows how their revenue and operating earnings (earnings before interest & taxes, or EBIT) stack up against one another.

Company B's unit volume is much higher given the high proportion of single-serve units sold, whereas Company A sells larger package sizes. Company A charges more per unit ($4 versus $0.25) and maintains better margins than Company B (12 percent versus 10 percent). This results in superior operating earnings for Company A. That's not the end of the story, however. Company B's business model has something going for it also—namely, efficient investment of capital.

Return on Capital Employed (ROCE) measures the efficiency and profitability of capital investments (similar to the Return on Invested Capital ratio). The calculation methodology is pretty straightforward: EBIT/Total Assets – Current Liabilities. Subtracting current liabilities from assets leaves equity and long-term liabilities (debt), or capital. This ratio is important because the real economic profit for any business is determined by how effectively it uses its capital (funds provided by lenders and investors to purchase physical capital, like equipment for producing goods and services). The better the returns using the least amount of capital the more a firm approaches optimality.

Table 6.1   Revenue Model Comparison

	Company A	Company B
Units Sold	75	800
$ Per Unit	$4	$0.25
Revenue	$300	$200
Operating Margin	12%	10%
EBIT	$36	$20

Simply, the economic environment of emerging markets requires firms to become more efficient to compete. How do they do this? Perhaps Company B will reduce its physical capital intensity by outsourcing production to dedicated suppliers rather than maintaining its own expensive plants and equipment. Other ways include implementing logistics and distribution strategies creating cost reduction, thus managing revenue in a manner reducing capital tied up in receivables (many firms collect revenues in real time as goods leave their suppliers' warehouses). Let's look at how our two companies compare in relation to ROCE.

$$ROCE = \frac{EBIT}{Total\ Assets - Current\ Liabilities}$$

Company A
$$ROCE = \frac{36}{40 - 5}$$
$$= \frac{36}{35}$$
$$= 103\%$$

Company B
$$ROCE = \frac{20}{25 - 10}$$
$$= \frac{20}{15}$$
$$= 133\%$$

Company B's business model exemplifies the blueprint for success used by many consumer product companies operating in EM. By employing less capital to achieve its operating profit relative to Company A, Company B has a higher ROCE and can make a viable case for emerging market expansion.

How might this business model come together? For starters, Company B outsources much of its production. This makes the firm less physically capital intensive (evidenced by total assets of 25 for Company B versus 40 for Company A). By keeping long-term debt low, Company B also employs less financial capital than Company A to generate proportionate earnings. The cumulative effect of these differences: *Company B has a higher return on capital despite having lower margins and operating earnings.* Such conditions are necessary to make a case for economic viability for an MNC operating in EM. Operating margins and revenues may pale in comparison to the developed world, but as long as firms judiciously manage their investment capital, they can still spawn efficient profits.

Another important feature of operating in EM: scale of production. Given the stringent price-performance equation and low margins per unit, high volume is a fundamental precept for return on investment. The largest MNCs operating in the largest EM countries (China, India, Brazil, and Mexico) meet these requirements most easily because they are able to make the necessary financial commitments to back successful innovations, generate mass distribution, and use scale to keep costs down and manage capital efficiently.

Different Natural Resource Standards   In the US, per capita use of water is around 1,932 cubic meters per year. That compares to 491 cubic meters in China and 640 cubic meters in India. This disparity requires MNCs to innovate new ways to provide functionality without depleting natural resources.[3]

For instance, Unilever is an example of an MNC with a strong presence in emerging markets, and it understands the unique requirements based on natural resource standards. Hindustan Unilever is India's largest consumer goods company and most prolific advertiser. One of the core strengths of the firm is its ability to cater to everyone among India's diverse population. For example, it makes several laundry detergents: Surf Excel for the affluent, Rin for the "aspiring" class, and Wheel for the poorer segments of society, many of whom live in the countryside.[4] Particularly in the countryside, products must succeed in the toughest conditions, including washing with little water, cold water, or even salt water. Some wash their clothes in river streams. A multinational corporation needs to understand these requirements. Unilever does and this is a reason why its Wheel detergent has been a success.

Water scarcity is not the only natural resource limitation consumer goods firms must consider. Electricity is also scarce and erratic. Blackouts are common and not all consumers have access to appliances like refrigerators. Executives at MNCs are therefore required to design very different products than those in the developed world if they are to serve these less developed regions effectively.

People in the developing world are exceptionally value conscious—they need to be. Consumers in Latin America, for instance, are known to be much more economical in their use of diapers, using only one or two per day on average. Because they can only afford one or two changes per day, they require diapers with a higher level of absorbency. Multinational corporations have responded to this challenge by producing higher-quality diapers specifically suited for these requirements.

Distribution

Not only must MNCs design innovative new ways to create what the developing world considers standard products to succeed in EMs, but they also must design unique modes of distribution.

Availability Multinational corporations must take into account where emerging market citizens live and their work patterns. Remember: Most consumers in this part of the world must work a full day before they have cash in hand to purchase that day's necessities. For this reason, stores selling consumer products usually stay open late and peak shopping times are after 7PM. Travel is another issue. Since many people do not have access to cars, stores must be within walking distance in many areas.

The Power of Distribution

Distribution has long been and continues to be a hurdle in emerging market country-sides, but the rapid rise of urban areas is making distribution easier. By 2015, over 368 cities in the developing world will each have more than 1 million residents. There will also be at least 23 cities with more than 10 million residents, each collectively accounting for between 1.5 and 2 billion people. Cities are the lowest-hanging fruit for consumer goods firms seeking emerging market expansion because distribution is more concentrated and urbanites tend to earn higher incomes, allowing them to more easily afford branded consumer products.

Source: CK Prahalad, *The Fortune at the Bottom of the Pyramid: Eradicating Poverty Through Profits,* (Wharton School Publishing, 2008), 12.

Direct Sales Networks   Direct sales is a popular tactic used in building distribution networks outside cities. For instance, Hindustan Unilever started a program to reach remote villages by enlisting the help of village women who are trained in distributing the company's products. The program is called Shakti, and it empowers women to become entrepreneurs by selling the firm's products within their local community. These women possess unique knowledge about what products are in demand in their villages, and they also educate their local communities on how to use the products they sell.

The cosmetics firm Avon, with its army of 800,000 "Avon ladies," has also been effective using a direct-sales model in EM, particularly in Brazil. Amway has had similar success in India, building a direct-distribution system that includes over 600,000 representatives providing a revenue base of $110 million.[5]

Building Distribution to Match Rapid Growth   In the developed world, the typical approach to diffusion of new consumer products resembles an "S" curve. New products are introduced early in the curve and take some time to gain traction. Once they've achieved resonance with consumers, distribution is scaled up over several years and the product is taken national. Years later, demand often begins to stagnate as new innovations with better functional benefits make their way in.[6]

In EM, a different type of curve forms with most consumer products—an "I" curve. Whereas the management process in most large firms in the developed world is geared toward slow growth, EM countries are expanding at a much quicker pace. The "I" curve means popular products can take off rapidly and make other products quickly obsolete.[7] This type of rapid-growth environment creates new demands for MNCs looking to quickly capture meaningful market share. Hindustan Unilever's goal is to quickly build a network of one million direct distributors. To achieve this, they must recruit and train between 30,000 and 40,000 people every month![8] Evaluating, hiring, and training this many applicants is a Herculean, but necessary, task if the firm is to beat competitors in gaining a strong foothold in a region with such a large population.

The "I" curve also poses new scaling challenges. Timing and the pace of distribution development become crucial. All the while, costs must be kept low to create capacity for consumption and overall market growth (consistent with Company B's business model profiled earlier).

Traditional "S Curve"

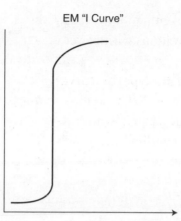

EM "I Curve"

Advertising

In the wealthier areas of emerging markets, advertising is not radically different than in the developed world. With the proliferation of cell phones, personal computers, radios, and televisions among urbanites, a large segment of emerging market consumers enjoy unprecedented access to information and entertainment. With these technologies comes mass advertising capability. Television has thus far been the most effective form of advertising in wealthier areas of emerging markets, where consumers tend to be very brand conscious. Particularly appealing are western aspirational brands (a person in the developing world may not be able to buy a BMW, but they can afford to buy "chic" western household products or beverages).

In poorer areas, however, most technologies we generally take for granted are not yet an option. For example, more than 40 percent of India is "media dark," so television and radio do not provide a medium to reach consumers and educate them on products. (Ads for consumer products in EM countries contain educative elements because many viewers have never used the products before.) More than two million children die each year from common ailments avoidable by simply washing one's hands. Hindustan Unilever uses this finding to educate potential new consumers. They often start by visiting village schools. They educate children on the causes of disease and how to prevent it, running simple demonstrations using ultraviolet dirt and bacteria detectors to show what "clean-looking hands" look like. The children become advocates and educate their families on the benefits of using Unilever's soap.[9]

Other common advertising strategies in media dark zones include billboards and truck-mounted demonstration crews whose catchy jingles attract large crowds in villages.

Speaking the Language

India has more than 15 official languages and 500 dialects, but 30 percent of the population is illiterate. These wide disparities complicate advertising and packaging design.

Source: CK Prahalad, *The Fortune at the Bottom of the Pyramid: Eradicating Poverty Through Profits,* (Wharton School Publishing, 2006), 25.

Market Penetration Strategies Kraft provides an example of advertising trial and error in the developing world. Oreo Cookies were first introduced in 1912 in the US, but it wasn't until 1996 that Oreos were launched in China. At first, sales were flat—Kraft researched why it was failing and found several key insights.

First, Kraft learned the Chinese were not big cookie eaters, and the US version of Oreos was too sweet for Chinese consumers. Kraft responded by testing different Oreo reformulations before arriving at the formula consumers thought tasted best. Also, the normal package sizes of 14 cookies were too expensive, so Kraft developed smaller packages, and the cost per pack fell.[10]

After reformulating and repackaging the product, Kraft revamped its marketing campaign. On the advice of its local Chinese marketing managers, the company tried a grassroots effort to educate the Chinese about the American tradition of cookies and milk. Tactics included recruiting Chinese university students to hand out free cookies and hold Oreo-themed basketball games. Next came TV commercials with kids dunking Oreo halves into milk.

Oreo sales accelerated, but Kraft still struggled to keep up with rival Nestlé—mainly because Nestlé sold chocolate-covered wafers, and China's wafer segment was growing faster than traditional biscuit-like cookies. Kraft introduced a new version of the Oreo—four layers of wafers, filled with vanilla and chocolate cream, coated in chocolate. This change was key—in 2006, Oreo wafer sticks became the best-selling biscuit in China. Kraft is now attempting to capitalize on its success by rolling out the wafers elsewhere in Asia. In the last two years, Kraft has doubled its Oreo revenue in China, pushing worldwide revenue from the brand to over the $1 billion mark for the first time.

Key takeaways

- Products popular in the developed world do not necessarily translate to the developing world. Often, products must be significantly reformulated to appeal to EM consumers. The right formulation can take years and extensive market research to uncover.
- Smaller, less expensive pack sizes are effective in EM. Most of the packaging sizes common in the developed world are too big and too expensive for EM consumers who often live on day-to-day budgets.
- Marketing consumer products effectively in the developing world requires creativity and outside-the-box thinking. Often, the chief marketing goal is to educate consumers about western practices of product use (e.g., cookies and milk). If consumers adopt the practice, it'll often happen in a way slightly different from the developed world based on their unique preferences and culture.

INVESTMENT IDIOSYNCRASIES

Much like the consumer goods executive who had to throw out the playbook he used in the developed world, you must relinquish some of your preconceived notions regarding Consumer Staples stocks when investing in emerging markets.

Know Your Audience

Wal-Mart has successfully expanded its presence in China but, like Kraft, quickly learned it had to tweak its product offerings. For instance, laundry detergent was initially a poor seller because many Chinese do not own a washing machine. Wal-Mart relayed this finding to P&G, who developed Tide hand wipes for washing laundry by hand. The product quickly became the best-selling detergent, selling 35,000 packages in 15 stores in the first two weeks.

Food offerings are also different in Chinese Wal-Mart stores, including displays for sushi, rotisserie chicken, and pig ears.

Source: David Faber, "The Age of Wal-Mart: Inside America's Most Powerful Company," documentary special report.

The developing world's growing manufacturing prowess has been widely covered in studies outside this book, so we will not do so here. Suffice it to say, many developing countries have comparative advantages allowing them to be low-cost producers for a wide array of manufactured goods, which they export to other developed nations. The EM story is no longer just about exporting, however—it's also about consumption and imports.

As middle- and lower-class folks in developing economies get better jobs, they receive better wages and have more disposable income. They spend new disposable income not only on discretionary items like electronics, but also on products we consider essentials. This includes products like soda, beer, snacks, cleaning supplies, and so on. Because a tipping point is required in disposable income for people to afford these items, Consumer Staples demand is more closely correlated to economic growth in emerging markets. In a recent research report, Goldman Sachs Global Investment Research identified a strong correlation between real GDP and Staples consumption in the BRICs from 1999 through 2007, citing an R^2 of 0.50.

Given Staples' higher degree of economic sensitivity in emerging markets, Staples stocks act a lot more like Consumer Discretionary when compared to the developed world. Table 6.2 shows the correlation between EM Consumer Staples performance versus EM

Table 6.2   Consumer Staples vs. Consumer Discretionary in the Developed World and Emerging Markets

	Correlation
MSCI World Consumer Staples vs. MSCI World Consumer Discretionary	0.25
MSCI EM Consumer Staples vs. MSCI EM Consumer Discretionary	0.78

Source: Thomson Datastream.

Consumer Discretionary, compared to the correlation of MSCI World Consumer Staples versus MSCI World Consumer Discretionary (based on monthly returns from 12/31/1998 through 12/31/2007).

To understand why Staples products behave more like Consumer Discretionary products in the developing world, we must revisit the notion of elasticity. Demand for Consumer Staples products are more income and price elastic in emerging markets than in developed countries. Thus, the sector is more economically sensitive. This trait should be kept top of mind when considering Consumer Staples investments in this part of the world.

Chapter Recap

The scale of the EM opportunity for Consumer Staples firms is immense. As large numbers of emerging market citizens continue to enter the middle class, they will increasingly adopt Consumer Staples products for the first time. This transformation provides powerful growth prospects in what is otherwise a mature industry where volume growth is difficult to come by.

- To be competitive, firms must create capacity to consume among the four billion people living on less than $2 a day by efficiently producing products at lower costs than in the developed world.
- Emerging market consumers live on day-to-day budgets, making single-serve packaging a popular model.

(Continued)

- The basic business model in emerging markets is small unit packages, low margin per unit, high volume, and high return on capital.
- Successful Consumer Staples firms in emerging markets understand the unique natural resource constrictions people face, including water and electricity scarcity, and they produce goods consistent with these requirements.
- Urbanization is making distribution for large MNCs easier.
- Direct sales is a common strategy to reach consumers living in distant villages.
- The rapid expansion in consumer product demand in emerging markets leads to a different kind of supply curve called an "I" curve, illustrating the need for firms to rapidly build distribution scale in order to seize meaningful market share.
- Advertising in emerging markets includes traditional methods like TV, radio, and Internet, as well as unique methods like demonstration crews that enter villages and teach people why and how they should use consumer products.
- The Consumer Staples sector acts more like Consumer Discretionary in EM due to a high correlation between economic growth and Consumer Staples consumption.

III

THINKING LIKE
A PORTFOLIO MANAGER

7

THE TOP-DOWN METHOD

So let's say you use what you have learned thus far to determine you are bullish on Consumer Staples. How much of your portfolio should you allocate to Consumer Staples stocks? Twenty-five percent? Fifty percent? One hundred percent? Most investors concern themselves only with individual companies ("I like Cadbury Schweppes, so I'll buy some") without considering how the stocks fit into their overall portfolio. But this is no way to manage your money.

In Part III of this book, we show you how to analyze the Consumer Staples sector like a top-down portfolio manager. This includes a full description of the top-down method, how to use benchmarks, and how the top-down method applies to the Consumer Staples sector. We then delve into security analysis, where we provide a framework for analyzing any company and discuss many of the important questions to ask when analyzing Consumer Staples firms. In the last chapter, we give a few examples of specific investing strategies for the sector.

INVESTING IS A SCIENCE

To be a great investor you have to develop a knack for anticipating the anticipations of others. There is no universally ordained playbook on how to do this consistently. Too many investors today think investing has "rules"—that all one must do to guarantee investing success for the long run is find the right set of investing rules. But that simply doesn't work. Why? Because all well-known and widely discussed information is already reflected in stock prices. This is a basic tenet of market theory and commonly referred to as *market efficiency*. So if you see a headline about a stock you follow, there's no use trading on that information—it's already priced in. You missed the move.

If everything known is already discounted in prices, the only way to beat the market is to know something others don't. Knowing something others don't is the root of all investment success not predicated on luck because that is the only method by which you can accurately anticipate the anticipations of others.

Now let's clarify an important point—access to information alone will not give you an edge on all of the other market participants. Think about it: There are countless intelligent investors and long-time professionals who fail to beat the market year after year, most with the same access to information as anyone else (if not more). What's the problem? It's not lack of information—rather, it's their lack of ability to critically analyze widely known information and form independent conclusions. Unique and correct analysis of widely known information is how you beat the stock market. Few people recall this simple fact in their day-to-day investing activities.

Most view investing as a craft. They think, "If I learn the craft of value investing and all its rules, then I can be a successful investor using that method." But that simply can't work because, by definition, all the conventional ways of thinking about value investing will already be widely known and thus priced in. Most investment styles are very well known and already widely practiced. There are undoubtedly millions of investors out there much like you, looking at the same metrics and information you are. So there isn't much power in them. Even the investing techniques themselves are widely known—taught to millions in universities and practiced by hundreds of thousands of professionals globally. There's no edge there.

Moreover, it's been demonstrated time and again investment styles move in and out of favor over time—no one style or category is inherently better than another in the long run. You may think "value" investing works wonders to beat markets, but the fact is "growth" stocks will trounce value at times.

One approach to beating stock markets lies in being dynamic—never adhering for all time to a single investment idea—and gleaning information the market hasn't yet priced in. In other words, you cannot adhere to a single set of "rules" and hope to outperform markets over time.

So how can you beat the markets? Start by thinking of investing as a science.

Einstein's Brain and the Stock Market

If he weren't so busy becoming the most renowned scientist of the twentieth century, Albert Einstein would have made a killing on Wall Street—but not because he had such a high IQ. Granted, he was immensely intelligent, but a high IQ alone does not a market guru make. (If it did, MIT professors would be making millions managing money instead of teaching.) Instead, it's the style of his thought and the method of his work that matter.

In the little we know about Einstein's investment track record, he didn't do very well. He lost most of his Nobel Prize money in bad bond ventures.[1] Heck, Sir Isaac Newton may have given us the three laws of motion, but even his talents didn't extend to investing. He lost his shirt in the South Sea Bubble of the early 1700s, explaining later, "I can calculate the movement of the stars, but not the madness of men."[2]

So why believe Einstein would have been a great portfolio manager if he put his mind to it? In short, Einstein was a true and highly creative scientist. He didn't take the acknowledged rules of physics as such—he used prior knowledge, logic, and creativity combined with the rigors of the verifiable, testable scientific method to create an entirely new view of the cosmos. In other words, he was dynamic and gleaned knowledge others didn't. Investors must do the same. (Not to worry, though, you won't need advanced calculus to do it.)

Einstein's unique character gave him an edge—he truly had a mind made to beat markets. Scientists have perused his work, his speeches, his letters, even his brain (literally) to find the secret of his intellect. In all, his approach to information processing and idea generation, his willingness to go against the grain of the establishment, and his relentless pursuit of answers to questions no one else was asking during his time ultimately made him a genius.

Most biographers and his contemporaries agree one of Einstein's foremost gifts was his ability to discern "the big picture." Unlike many scientists who could easily drown themselves in data minutiae, Einstein had an ability to see above the fray. Another way to say this is he could take the same information everyone else in his time was looking at and interpret it differently, yet correctly. He accomplished this by using his talent for extracting the most important data from what he studied and linking them together in innovative ways no one else could.

Einstein called this *combinatory play*. Similar to a child experimenting with a new Lego set, Einstein would combine and recombine seemingly unrelated ideas, concepts, and images to produce new, original discoveries. In the end, most all new ideas are merely the combination of existing ones in one form or another. Take $E = mc^2$: Einstein was not the first to discover the concepts of energy, mass, or the speed of light; rather, he combined these concepts in a novel way and, in the process, altered the way we view the universe.[3]

Einstein's combinatory play is a terrific metaphor for stock investing. To be a successful market strategist, you must be able to extract the most important data items from all of the "noise" permeating today's markets and generate conclusions the market hasn't yet appreciated. Central to this task is your ability to link these data items together in unique ways to produce new insights and themes for your portfolio.

Einstein learned the basics of science just like his peers. But once he had those mastered he directed his brain to challenging prior assumptions and inventing entirely different lenses to look through.

This is why this book isn't intended to give you a "silver bullet" for picking the right Consumer Staples stocks. The fact is the "right" stocks will be different in different times and situations. You don't have to be Einstein, you just have to think differently (and like a scientist) if you want to beat markets.

THE TOP-DOWN METHOD

Overwhelmingly, investment professionals today do what can broadly be labeled as "bottom-up" investing. Their emphasis is stock selection. A typical bottom-up investor researches an assortment of companies and attempts to pick those with the greatest likelihood of outperforming the market based on individual merits. The selected securities are cobbled together to form a portfolio, and factors like country and economic sector exposures are purely residuals of security selection, not planned decisions.

"Top-down" investing reverses the order of operations. A top-down investor first analyzes big picture factors like economics, politics, and sentiment to forecast which investment categories are most likely to outperform the market. Only then, and within those categories, does the top-down investor begin to look at individual securities. Top-down investing is inevitably more concerned with a portfolio's aggregate exposure to investment categories and factors than with any individual security. Thus, top-down is an inherently *dynamic* mode of investing because investment strategies are based upon the prevailing market and economic environment (which changes often).

There is significant debate in the investment community as to which approach is superior. This book's goal is not to reject bottom-up investing—there are indeed investors who've successfully utilized bottom-up approaches. Rather, the goal is to introduce a comprehensive and flexible methodology that any investor could employ to build a portfolio designed to beat the global stock market in any investment environment. It's a framework for gleaning new insights and making good on information not already reflected in stock prices.

Before we describe the method, let's explore several key reasons why a top-down approach is advantageous:

- **Scalability:** A bottom-up process is like looking for needles in a haystack. A top-down process is like looking for the haystack with the highest concentration of needles. There are nearly 25,000 publicly traded stocks globally. Even the largest institutions with the greatest research resources cannot hope to adequately examine all these companies. Smaller institutions and individual investors must necessarily prioritize where to focus their limited resources. Unlike a bottom-up process, a top-down process makes this gargantuan task manageable by determining upfront what slices of the market to examine at the security level.
- **Enhanced Stock Selection:** Well-designed top-down processes generate insights that can greatly enhance stock selection. Macro-economic or political analysis, for instance, can help determine what types of strategic attributes will face head- or tailwinds (see Chapter 8 for a full explanation).
- **Risk Control:** Bottom-up processes are highly subject to unintended risk concentrations. Top-down processes are inherently better suited to manage risk exposures throughout the investment process.
- **Macro Overview:** Top-down processes are more conducive to avoiding macro-driven calamities like the bursting of the Japan bubble in the 1990s, the Technology bubble in 2000, or the bear market of 2000 to 2002. No matter how good an individual company may be, it is still beholden to sector, regional, and broader market factors. In fact, there is evidence "macro" factors can largely determine a stock's performance regardless of individual merit.

Top-Down Means Thinking 70-20-10

A top-down investment process also helps focus on what's most important to investment results: asset allocation and sub-asset allocation decisions. Many investors focus most of their attention on security-level portfolio decisions such as picking individual stocks they think will perform well. However, studies have shown that over 90 percent of the variability in return is derived from asset allocation decisions,[4] not market timing or stock selection.

Our research shows about 70 percent of the variability in returns is derived from asset allocation, 20 percent from sub-asset allocation (such as country, sector, size, style), and 10 percent from security selection. So while security selection can make a significant difference over time, more often than not, higher level portfolio decisions dominate investment results.

The balance of this chapter defines the various steps in the top-down method, specifically as they relate to making country, sector, and style decisions. This same basic framework can be applied to portfolios to make allocations within sectors. At the end of the chapter, we detail how this framework can be applied to the Consumer Staples sector.

Benchmarks

A key facet of the top-down model is utilizing benchmarks. A benchmark is typically a broad-based index of securities like the S&P 500, MSCI World, or Russell 2000. Benchmarks are indispensable roadmaps for structuring a portfolio, monitoring risk, and judging performance over time.

Tactically, a portfolio should be structured to maximize the probability of consistently beating the benchmark. This is inherently different than maximizing returns. Unlike aiming to achieve some fixed rate of return each year, which will cause disappointment when your chosen asset class is very strong and is potentially unrealistic when it's very weak, a properly benchmarked portfolio provides a realistic guide for dealing with uncertain market conditions.

Portfolio construction begins by evaluating the characteristics of the chosen benchmark: sector weights, country weights, and market cap and valuations. Then an expected risk and return is assigned to each of these segments (based on portfolio drivers) and the areas most attractive are overweighted, while the least attractive are underweighted. Table 7.1 shows the MSCI World Index sector characteristics as of December 31, 2007 as an example, while Table 7.2 shows country characteristics, and Table 7.3 shows market cap and valuations.

Based on benchmark characteristics, portfolio drivers are then used to determine country, sector, and style decisions for the portfolio. For example, the Financials sector weight in the MSCI World Index is about 23 percent. Therefore, a portfolio managed against this benchmark would consider a 23 percent weight in Financials "neutral," or market weighted. If you believe Financials will perform better than the market in the foreseeable future, then you would "overweight" the sector, or carry a percentage of stocks in your portfolio greater than 23 percent. The reverse is true for an "underweight," where you'd hold less than 23 percent in Financials if you were pessimistic on the sector looking ahead.

Note that being pessimistic on Financials *doesn't necessarily mean holding zero Financials stocks.* It might only mean holding a lesser percentage of stocks in your portfolio than the benchmark. This is an important feature of benchmarking—it allows an investor to make strategic decisions on sectors and countries but maintains diversification, thus managing risk more appropriately.

Table 7.1   MSCI World Characteristics—Sectors

Sector	Weight
Financials	22.6%
Industrials	11.4%
Information Technology	11.0%
Energy	10.9%
Consumer Discretionary	9.8%
Consumer Staples	8.8%
Health Care	8.7%
Materials	7.2%
Telecommunication	4.9%
Utilities	4.7%

Source: Thomson Datastream; MSCI, Inc.[5] as of 12/31/07.

Table 7.2   MSCI World Characteristics—Countries

Country	Weight
US	47.1%
UK	10.8%
Japan	9.7%
France	5.2%
Germany	4.6%
Canada	4.1%
Switzerland	3.3%
Australia	3.2%
Spain	2.1%
Italy	1.9%
Netherlands	1.4%
Hong Kong	1.2%
Sweden	1.1%
Finland	0.9%
Belgium	0.6%
Singapore	0.5%
Norway	0.5%
Denmark	0.5%
Greece	0.4%
Ireland	0.3%
Austria	0.3%
Portugal	0.2%
New Zealand	0.1%
Emerging Markets	0.0%

Source: Thomson Datastream; MSCI, Inc.[6] as of 12/31/07.

Broad benchmarks are most useful for overall portfolio management. But sector-specific benchmarks for portions of portfolios can be useful in analyzing relative weights of industry groups, industries, and sub-industries within each sector. For the Consumer Staples sector, we can use indexes like the S&P 500 Consumer Staples, MSCI World Consumer Staples, or Russell 2000 Consumer Staples indexes. The components of these benchmarks can then be evaluated at a more detailed level.

Table 7.3   MSCI World Characteristics—Market Cap and Valuations

	Valuations
Median Market Cap	$7.3 Billion
Weighted Average Market Cap	$80.9 Billion
P/E	15.5
P/B	2.6
Div Yield	2.3
P/CF	12.7
P/S	2.4
Number of Holdings	1959

Source: Thomson Datastream; MSCI, Inc.[7] as of 12/31/07.

TOP-DOWN DECONSTRUCTED

The top-down method begins by first analyzing the macro environment and determining drivers. *Drivers* are specific indicators you can use to make portfolio management decisions. A collection of drivers can add up to generalized themes that help to answer the "big" questions like: Do you think stocks will go up or down in the next 12 months? If so, which countries or sectors should benefit most? Once you have decided on high-level portfolio drivers, you can examine additional macroeconomic portfolio drivers to make general overweight and underweight decisions for countries, sectors, industries, and sub-industries versus your benchmark.

For instance, let's say we've determined a macroeconomic theme that goes something like this, "In the next 12 months, I believe global economic growth will be weaker than most expect." That's a very high-level statement with important implications for your portfolio. It means you'd want to search for stocks that would perform best in a weakening demand environment.

The second step in top-down is to apply quantitative screening criteria to narrow the choice set of stocks. Since we believe, in our hypothetical example, that global growth will slow, it likely means we're bullish on Consumer Staples stocks given their "safe haven" appeal. But which ones? Should we be bullish on, say, beverages? Household product companies? Do we want small-cap Staples companies in our portfolio or large cap? And what about valuations? Should we be targeting growth or value? (Size and growth/value categories are often referred to as "style" decisions.) These criteria and more can help you narrow the list of stocks you might buy.

The third and final step is to perform fundamental analysis on individual stocks. Notice that a great deal of thinking, analysis, and work is done before you ever even think about individual stocks. That's the key to the top-down approach: It emphasizes high-level themes and funnels its way down to individual stocks.

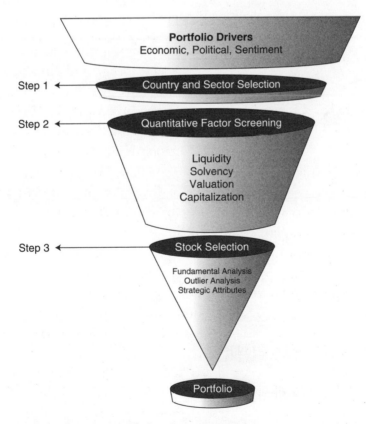

Figure 7.1   Portfolio Drivers

Step 1: Analyze Portfolio Drivers and Country and Sector Selection

Let's examine the first step in the top-down method more closely. In order to make top-down decisions, we develop and analyze what we call *portfolio drivers* (mentioned previously). We segment these portfolio drivers in three general categories: *economic, political,* and *sentiment.*

Portfolio drivers are what drive the performance of a broad category of stocks. Accurately identifying current and future drivers will help you find areas of the market most likely to outperform or underperform your benchmark (i.e., the broader stock market).

Table 7.4 shows examples of each type of portfolio driver. It's important to note these drivers are by no means comprehensive nor are they valid for all time periods. In fact, correctly identifying new portfolio drivers is essential to beating the market in the long term.

Economic Drivers   *Economic drivers* are anything related to the macroeconomic environment. This could include monetary policy,

Table 7.4   Portfolio Driver Examples

Economic	Political	Sentiment
Yield Curve Spread	Taxation	Mutual Fund Flows
Relative GDP Growth	Property Rights	Relative Style and Asset Class Valuations
Monetary Base/Growth	Structural Reform	Media Coverage
Currency Strength	Privatization	Institutional Searches
Relative Interest Rates	Trade/Capital Barriers	Consumer Confidence
Inflation	Current Account	Foreign Investment
Debt Level (Sovereign, Corporate, Consumer)	Government Stability	Professional Investor Forecasts
Infrastructure Spending	Political Turnover	Momentum Cycle Analysis
M&A, Issuance, and Repurchase Activity	Wars/Conflicts	Risk Aversion

interest rates, lending activity, yield curve analysis, relative GDP growth analysis, and myriad others. What economic forces are likely to drive GDP growth in countries around the world? What is the outlook for interest rates and how would that impact sectors? What is the outlook for technology and infrastructure spending among countries?

Economic drivers pertain not only to the fundamental outlook of the economy (GDP growth, interest rates, inflation), but also to the stock market (valuations, M&A activity, share buybacks). As an investor, it's your job to identify these drivers and determine how they'll impact your portfolio and each of its segments.

The following is an example list of economic drivers that could impact portfolio performance:

- US economic growth will be higher than consensus expectations.
- European Union interest rates will remain benign.
- Mergers, acquisitions, and share buybacks will remain strong.
- Emerging markets growth will drive commodity demand.

Political Drivers   Political drivers can be country-specific, pertain to regions (European Union, OECD), or affect interaction between countries or regions (such as trade policies). These drivers are more concerned with categories such as taxation, government stability, fiscal policy, and political turnover. Which countries are experiencing a change in government that could have a meaningful impact on their economies? Which sectors could be at risk from new taxation or legislation? Which countries are undergoing pro-growth reforms?

Political drivers will help determine the relative attractiveness of market segments and countries based on the outlook for the political environment. Most investors suffer from "home country bias," where they ascribe too much emphasis to the politics of their own countries. Always keep in mind it's a big, interconnected world out there, and geopolitical developments everywhere can have implications.

What are possible political drivers you can find? The following is a list of examples that can drive stocks up or down.

- Political party change in Japan driving pro-growth reforms.
- New tax policies in Germany stalling economic growth.
- Protests, government coups, and conflict driving political instability in Thailand.

Sentiment Drivers   Sentiment drivers attempt to measure consensus thinking about investment categories. Ideally, drivers identify market opportunities where sentiment is different than reality. For example, let's say you observe broad market sentiment currently expects a US recession in the next year. But you disagree and believe GDP growth will be strong. This presents an excellent opportunity for excess returns. You can load up on stocks that will benefit from an economic boom and watch the prices rise as the rest of the market realizes it later.

Since the market is a discounter of all widely known information, it's important to try and identify what the market is pricing in. The interpretation of such investor drivers is typically counter-intuitive (avoid what is overly popular and seek what is largely unpopular). Which sectors are investors most bullish about looking forward and why? What countries or sectors are widely discussed in the media? What market segments have been bid up recently based on something other than fundamentals? If the market's perception is different than fundamentals in the short term, stocks will eventually correct themselves to reflect reality in the long term.

A note of caution: Gauging market sentiment does not mean being a *contrarian*. Contrarians are investors who simply do the opposite of what most believe will happen. Instead, find places where sentiment (people's beliefs) doesn't match what you believe is reality and position your portfolio accordingly.

Examples of sentiment drivers include:

- Investors remain pessimistic about Technology despite improving fundamentals.
- Sentiment for the Chinese stock market is approaching euphoria, stretching valuations.

- Professional investors universally forecast US small-cap stocks to outperform, indicating demand for small caps has nowhere to go but down.

How to Create Your Own Investment Drivers

In order to form your own investment drivers, the first step is accessing a wide array of data from multiple sources. For country drivers, this could range from globally focused publications like the *Wall Street Journal* or *Financial Times* to regional newspapers or government data. For sector drivers, this could include reading trade publications or following major company announcements.

Remember, however, that markets are efficient—they reflect all widely known information. Most pertinent information about public companies is, well, *public*. Which means the market already knows. News travels fast, and markets absorb the knowledge and expectations of investors very quickly. Those seeking to profit on a bit of news, rumor, or speculation must acknowledge the market will probably move faster than they can. Therefore, in order to consistently generate excess returns, you must either know something others don't or interpret widely known information differently and correctly from the crowd. (For a detailed discussion on these factors and more, read *The Only Three Questions That Count* by Ken Fisher.)

Step 2: Quantitative Factor Screening

Step two in the top-down method is screening for quantitative factors. With your portfolio drivers in place, this allows you to narrow the potential list of stocks.

There are thousands and thousands of stocks out there, so it's vital to use a series of factors like market capitalization and valuations to narrow the field a bit. Securities passing this screen are then subjected to further quantitative analysis that eliminates companies with excessive risk profiles relative to their peer group (such as companies with excessive leverage or balance sheet risk) and securities lacking sufficient liquidity for investment.

The rigidity of the quantitative screens is entirely up to you and will determine the number of companies on your prospect list.

The more rigid the criteria, the fewer the companies that make the list. Broader criteria will increase the number of companies.

How might you define such a screen? Here are two examples of quantitative factor screenings, one using strict criteria and one that is broader.

Strict Criteria

- First, you decide you want to search for companies in the Consumer Staples sector only. By definition, that excludes all companies from the other nine sectors. Already, you've narrowed the field a lot!
- Now, let's say you want European Consumer Staples stocks only. By excluding all other regions besides Europe, you've narrowed the field even more.
- Next, let's decide to search only for Food & Staples Retailing companies in the sector.
- Perhaps you don't believe very small stocks are preferable, so you limit market capitalization to $5 billion and above.
- Last, let's set some valuation parameters:
  - P/E (price to earnings) less than 15x
  - P/B (price to book) less than 4x
  - P/CF (price to cash flow) less than 10x
  - P/S (price to sales) less than 2x

This rigorous process of selecting parameters will yield a small number of stocks to research, all based upon our higher level themes.

Now, what if you have reason to be less specific and want to do a broader screen because you think Consumer Staples in general is a good place to be?

Broad Criteria

- Consumer Staples sector
- Global (no country or region restrictions)
- Market caps above $10 billion

This selection process is much broader and obviously gives you a much longer list of stocks to choose from. Doing either a strict or a broad screen isn't inherently better. It just depends on how well-informed and specific your higher level themes are. Obviously, a stricter screen means less work for you in Step 3—actual stock selection.

Step 3: Stock Selection

After narrowing the prospect list, your final step is identifying individual securities that possess strategic attributes consistent with higher level portfolio themes. (We'll cover the stock selection process specifically in more detail in Chapter 8.) Your stock selection process should attempt to accomplish two goals:

1. Seek firms possessing strategic attributes consistent with higher level portfolio themes, derived from the drivers that give those firms a competitive advantage versus their peers. For example, if you believe owning firms with dominant market shares in consolidating industries is a favorable characteristic, you would search for companies with that profile.
2. Seek to maximize the likelihood of beating the category of stocks you are analyzing. For example, if you want a certain portfolio weight of packaged food companies and need 4 stocks out of 12 meeting the quantitative criteria, you then pick the 4 that, as a group, maximize the likelihood of beating all 12 as a whole. This is different than trying to pick "the best four." By avoiding stocks likely to be extreme or "weird" outliers versus the group, you can reduce portfolio risk while adding value at the security selection level.

In lieu of picking individual securities, there are other ways to exploit high-level themes in the top-down process. For instance, if you feel strongly about a particular sub-industry but don't think you can add value through individual security analysis, it may be more prudent to buy a group of companies in the sub-industry or via a category product like an exchange traded fund (ETF). For more information on

ETFs, visit www.ishares.com or www.sectorspdr.com. This way, you can be sure to gain broad sub-industry exposure without much stock-specific risk.

MANAGING AGAINST A CONSUMER STAPLES BENCHMARK

Now we can practice translating this specifically to your Consumer Staples allocation. Just as you analyze the components of your benchmark to determine country and sector components in a top-down strategy, you must analyze each sector's components, as we did in Chapter 4. To demonstrate how, we'll use the MSCI World Consumer Staples Sector index as the benchmark. Table 7.5 shows the MSCI World Consumer Staples industry weights as of December 31, 2007. We don't know what the sample portfolio weights should be, but we know it should add up to 100 percent. Of course, if managing against a broader benchmark, your Consumer Staples sector weight may add up to more or less than the Consumer Staples weight in the benchmark, depending on over- or underweight decisions.

Keeping the industry weights in mind will help mitigate benchmark risk. If you have a portfolio of stocks with the same industry

Table 7.5   MSCI World Materials Industry Weights vs. Sample Portfolio

Industry	MSCI World	Sample Portfolio
Food & Staples Retailing	24.9%	?
Food	24.8%	?
Beverages	20.3%	?
Household Products	14.3%	?
Tobacco	12.8%	?
Personal Products	3.0%	?
Total	100.0%	100.0%

Source: Thomson Datastream; MSCI, Inc.[8] as of 12/31/07.

weights as the MSCI World Consumer Staples Index, you're *neutral* from an industry standpoint. However, if you feel strongly about an industry, like Personal Products, and decide to only purchase those firms (one of the smallest weights in the sector), you're taking a huge benchmark risk. The same is true if you significantly *underweight* an industry. All the same rules apply as when you do this from a broader portfolio perspective, as we did earlier this chapter.

The benchmark industry weights provide a jumping-off point in making further portfolio decisions. Once you make higher-level decisions on the sub-industries, you can make choices versus the benchmark by overweighting the industries you feel likeliest to perform best and underweighting those likeliest to perform worst. Table 7.6 shows how you can make different portfolio bets against the benchmark by over- and underweighting industries.

Note: Portfolio A might be a portfolio of all Consumer Staples stocks, or it can simply represent a neutral Consumer Staples sector allocation in a larger portfolio.

The "difference" column shows the relative difference between the benchmark and Portfolio A. In this example, Portfolio A is most overweight to Food and most underweight to Food & Staples Retailing.

In other words, for this hypothetical example, Portfolio A's owner expects Food to outperform the sector and Food & Staples Retailing

Table 7.6   Portfolio A

Industry	MSCI World	Portfolio A	Difference
Food & Staples Retailing	24.9%	16.0%	−8.9%
Food	24.8%	34.0%	9.2%
Beverages	20.3%	24.0%	3.7%
Household Products	14.3%	20.1%	5.8%
Tobacco	12.8%	6.0%	−6.8%
Personal Products	3.0%	0.0%	−3.0%
Total	100.0%	100.0%	0.0%

Source: Thomson Datastream; MSCI, Inc.[9] as of 12/31/07.

to underperform the sector. But in terms of benchmark risk, Portfolio A remains fairly close to the benchmark weights, so its relative risk is quite modest. This is extremely important: By managing against a benchmark, you can make strategic choices to beat the index without concentrating too heavily in a specific area, and you are also well diversified within the sector.

Table 7.7 is another example of relative portfolio weighting versus the benchmark. Portfolio B is significantly underweight to Food & Staples Retailing, with zero exposure, and very overweight to Food. Because the industry weights are so different from the benchmark, Portfolio B takes on substantially more relative risk versus A.

Regardless of how your portfolio is positioned relative to a benchmark, it's important to use benchmarks to identify where your relative risks are before investing. Knowing the benchmark weights and having opinions on the future performance of each sub-industry is a crucial step in building a portfolio designed to beat the benchmark. Should you make the correct overweight and underweight decisions, you're likelier to beat the benchmark, regardless of the individual securities held within. But even if you're wrong, you'll have diversified enough not to underperform your benchmark by a wide margin.

Which again brings us to picking individual stocks, and Chapter 8.

Table 7.7   Portfolio B

Industry	MSCI World	Portfolio B	Difference
Food & Staples Retailing	24.9%	0.0%	−24.9%
Food	24.8%	60.0%	35.2%
Beverages	20.3%	22.0%	1.7%
Household Products	14.3%	12.1%	−2.2%
Tobacco	12.8%	6.0%	−6.8%
Personal Products	3.0%	0.0%	−3.0%
Total	100.0%	100.0%	0.0%

Source: Thomson Datastream; MSCI, Inc.[10] as of 12/31/07.

Chapter Recap

A more effective approach to sector analysis is "top-down." A top-down investment methodology analyzes big-picture factors such as economic, political, and sentiment drivers to forecast which investment categories are likely to outperform the market. A key part of the process is the use of benchmarks (like the MSCI World Consumer Staples or S&P 500 Consumer Staples indexes), which are used as guides for building portfolios, monitoring performance, and managing risk. By analyzing portfolio drivers, we can identify which Consumer Staples industries and sub-industries are most attractive and unattractive, ultimately filtering down to stock selection.

- The top-down investment methodology first identifies and analyzes high-level portfolio drivers affecting broad categories of stocks. These drivers help determine portfolio country, sector, and style weights. The same methodology can be applied to a specific sector to determine industry and sub-industry weights.
- Quantitative factor screening helps narrow the list of potential portfolio holdings based on characteristics such as valuations, liquidity, and solvency.
- Stock selection is the last step in the top-down process. Stock selection attempts to find companies possessing strategic attributes consistent with higher level portfolio drivers.
- Stock selection also attempts to find companies with the greatest probability of outperforming their peers.
- It's helpful to use a Consumer Staples benchmark as a guide when constructing a portfolio to determine your sub-industry overweights and underweights.

8

SECURITY ANALYSIS

Now that we've covered the top-down method, let's pick some stocks. This chapter walks you through analyzing individual Consumer Staples firms using the top-down method presented in Chapter 7. Specifically, we'll demonstrate a five-step process for analyzing firms relative to peers.

Every firm and every stock is different, but viewing them through the right lens is vital. Investors need a functional, consistent, and reusable framework for analyzing securities across the sector. While by no means comprehensive, the framework provided and the questions at this chapter's end should serve as good starting points to help identify strategic attributes and company-specific risks.

While volumes have been written about individual security analysis, a top-down investment approach de-emphasizes the importance of stock selection in a portfolio. As such, we'll talk about the basics of stock analysis for the beginning to intermediate investor. For a more thorough understanding of financial statement analysis, valuations, modeling, and other tools of security analysis, additional reading is suggested.

> ### Top-Down Recap
>
> As covered in Chapter 7, you can use the top-down method to make your biggest, most important portfolio decisions first. However, the same process applies when picking stocks, and those high-level portfolio decisions ultimately filter down to individual securities.
>
> Step 1 is analyzing the broader global economy and identifying various macro "drivers" affecting the entire sector or industry. Using the drivers, you can make general allocation decisions for countries, sectors, industries, and sub-industries versus the given benchmark. Step 2 is applying quantitative screening criteria to narrow the choice set of stocks. It's not until all those decisions are made that we get to analyze individual stocks. Security analysis is the third and final step.
>
> For the rest of the chapter, we assume you have already established a benchmark, solidified portfolio themes, made sub-industry overweight and underweight decisions, and are ready to analyze firms within a peer group. (A *peer group* is a group of stocks you'd generally expect to perform similarly because they operate in the same industry, possibly share the same geography, and have similar quantitative attributes.)

MAKE YOUR SELECTION

Security analysis is nowhere near as complicated as it may seem—but that doesn't mean it's easy. Similar to your goal in choosing industry and sector weights, you've got one basic task: spot opportunities not currently discounted into prices. Or, put differently, know something others don't. Investors should analyze firms by taking consensus expectations for a company's estimated financial results and then assessing whether it will perform below, inline, or above those baseline expectations. Profit opportunities arise when your expectations are different and more accurate than consensus expectations. Trading on widely known information or consensus expectations adds no value to the stock selection process. Doing so is no different than trading on a coin flip.

The top-down method offers two ways to spot such opportunities. First, accurately predict high-level, macro themes affecting an industry or group of companies—these are your portfolio drivers. Second, find firms that will benefit *most* if those high-level themes and drivers play out. This is done by finding firms with *competitive advantages* (we'll explain this concept more in a bit).

Since the majority of excess return is added in higher level decisions in the top-down process, it's not vital to pick the "best" stocks in the universe. Rather, you want to pick stocks with a good probability of outperforming their peers. Doing so can enhance returns without jeopardizing good top-down decisions by picking risky, go-big-or-go-home stocks. Being right more often than not should create outperformance relative to the benchmark over time.

A FIVE-STEP PROCESS

Analyzing a stock against its peer group can be summarized in a five-step process:

1. Understand business and earnings drivers.
2. Identify strategic attributes.
3. Analyze fundamental and stock price performance.
4. Identify risks.
5. Analyze valuations and consensus expectations.

These five steps provide a consistent framework for analyzing firms in their peer groups. While these steps are far from a full stock analysis, they provide the basics necessary to begin making better stock selections.

Step 1: Understand Business and Earnings Drivers

The first step is to understand what the firm does, how it generates its earnings, and what drives those earnings. Here are a few tips to help in the process.

- **Industry overview:** Begin any analysis with a basic understanding of the firm's industry, including its drivers and risks. You should be familiar with how current economic trends affect the industry.

- **Company description:** Obtain a business description of the company, including an understanding of the products and services within each business segment. It's always best to go directly to a company's financial statements for this. (Almost every public firm makes their financial statements readily accessible online these days.) Browse the firm's website and financial statements/reports to gain an overview of the company and how it presents itself.

- **Corporate history:** Read the firm's history since its inception. An understanding of firm history may reveal its growth strategy or consistency with success and failure. It also will provide clues on what its true core competencies are. Ask questions like: Has it been an industry leader for decades, or is it a relative newcomer? Has it switched strategies or businesses often in the past?

- **Business segments:** Break down company revenues and earnings by business segment and geography to determine how and where revenue is derived. Find out what drives results in each business and geographic segment. Begin thinking about how each of these business segments fits into your high-level themes. You can usually find this information in the most recent 10-K filing.

- **Recent news/press releases:** Read all recent news about the stock, including press releases. Do an Internet search and see what comes up. Look for any significant announcements regarding company operations. What is the media's opinion of the firm?

- **Markets and customers:** Identify the firm's main customers and the markets it operates in. Determine if the firm has any particularly large single customer or a concentrated customer base. This information can usually be accessed via the 10-K.

- **Competition:** Find the main competitors and how market share compares with other industry players. Is it highly segmented? Assess the industry's competitive landscape. Keep in mind the biggest competitors can sometimes lurk in different industries—sometimes even in different sectors! Get a feel for how it stacks up—is it an industry leader or a minor player? Does market share matter in that industry? Reading industry reports and researching competitors are good ways to get a handle on the competitive landscape.

Step 2: Identify Strategic Attributes

After gaining a firm grasp of firm operations, the next step is identifying strategic attributes consistent with higher level portfolio themes. Also known as *competitive* or *comparative advantages*, strategic attributes are unique features that allow firms to outperform their industry or sector. As industry peers are generally affected by the same high-level drivers, strong strategic attributes are the edge in creating superior outperformance. Examples of strategic attributes include:

- High relative market share
- Low-cost producer
- Sales relationships/distribution
- Economic sensitivity
- Vertical integration
- Management/business strategy
- Geographic diversity or advantage
- Consolidator
- Strong balance sheet
- Niche markets
- Pure play
- Potential takeover target
- Proprietary technologies
- Strong brand name
- First mover advantage

Portfolio drivers help determine which strategic attributes are likely to face head- or tailwinds. After all, not all strategic attributes will benefit a firm in all environments. For example, while higher operating leverage might help a firm boost earnings when the industry is booming, it would have the opposite effect in a down cycle. A pertinent

Strategic Attributes: Making Lemonade

How do strategic attributes help you analyze individual stocks? Consider a simple example: There are five lemonade stands of similar size, product, and quality all within a city block. A scorching heat wave envelops the city, sending a rush of customers in search of lemonade. Which stand benefits most from the industry-wide surge in business? This likely depends on each stand's strategic attributes. Maybe one is a cost leader and has cheapest access to homegrown lemons. Maybe one has a geographic advantage and is located next to a basketball court full of thirsty players. Or maybe one has a superior business strategy with a "buy two, get one free" initiative that drives higher sales volume and a bigger customer base. Any of these is a core strategic advantage.

Consumer Staples example could be exposure to emerging markets. This exposure is beneficial only as long as the emerging markets it operates in are growing healthily. However, if inflation begins to run rampant and leads to a severe pullback in emerging markets consumption, firms with a lot of exposure to the markets and tough year-over-year comps could see a drag on earnings growth relative to other producers. Thus, it's essential to pick strategic attributes consistent with higher level portfolio themes and be dynamic in stock selection as those themes and attributes change.

A strategic attribute is also only effective to the extent management recognizes and takes advantage of it. Execution is important. For example, if a firm's strategic attribute is technological expertise, it should focus its effort on research and development to maintain that edge. If its strategic attribute is being a low-cost producer within its peer group, it should capitalize by potentially lowering prices or expanding production (assuming the new production is also low cost) to gain market share.

Identifying strategic attributes may require thorough research of the firm's financial statements, website, news stories, history, and discussions with customers, suppliers, competitors, or management. Don't skimp on this step—be diligent and thorough in finding strategic attributes. It may feel like an arduous task at times, but it's also among the most important steps in security selection.

Step 3: Analyze Fundamental and Stock Price Performance

Once you've gained a thorough understanding of the business, earnings drivers, and strategic attributes, the next step is analyzing firm performance both fundamentally and in the stock market.

Using the latest earnings releases and annual report, analyze company performance in recent quarters. Ask the following questions:

- What are recent revenue trends? Earnings? Margins? Which business segments are seeing rising or falling sales?
- Is the firm growing its business organically, because of acquisitions, or some other method?
- How sustainable is the firm's strategy?
- Are earnings growing because of strong demand or because of cost cutting?
- Is it benefiting from tax loopholes or one-time items?
- What is management's strategy to grow the business for the future?
- What is the financial health of the company?

Not all earnings results are created equal. Understanding what drives results will give clues to what drives future performance.

Check the company's stock chart for the last few years and try to determine what has driven performance. Explain any big up or down moves and identify any significant news events. If the stock price has trended steadily downward despite consistently beating earnings estimates, there may be a force driving the whole industry down, like rising input costs. Likewise, if the company's stock soared despite reporting tepid earnings growth or prospects, there may be some force driving the industry higher, like takeover speculation. Or stocks can simply move in sympathy with the broader market. Whatever it is, make sure you know.

After reading the earnings calls of a firm and its peers (these are typically posted on the Investor Relations section of a firm's website every quarter), you'll begin to notice similar trends and events affecting the industry. Take note of these so you can distinguish between issues that are company specific or industrywide. For example, economic growth affects entire Consumer Staples industries, but hedging policies or an individual government's tax policies may only affect specific producers.

Step 4: Identify Risks

There are two main types of risk in security analysis: stock-specific risk and systematic risk (also known as non–stock specific risk). Both can be equally important to performance.

Stock-specific risks, as the name suggests, are issues affecting the company in isolation. These are mainly risks affecting a firm's business operations. Some company-specific risks are discussed in detail in the 10-K for US firms and the 20-F for foreign filers (found at www.sec .gov). But one can't rely solely on firms self-identifying their risk factors. You must see what analysts are saying about them and identify all risks for yourself. Some examples include:

- Stock ownership concentration (insider or institutional)
- Customer concentration
- Poor corporate governance
- Excessive leverage or lack of access to financing
- Obsolete products
- Poor operational track record
- High cost of products versus competitors
- Late Securities and Exchange Commission (SEC) filings
- Qualified audit opinions
- Unsound hedging activities
- Pension or benefit underfunding risk
- Regulatory or legal (e.g., pending litigation)
- Pending corporate actions
- Executive departures

Systematic risks include macroeconomic or geopolitical events out of a company's control. While the risks may affect a broad set of firms, they will have varying effects on each. Some examples include:

- Industry cost inflation
- Economic activity
- Geopolitical risks
- Legislation affecting taxes, royalties, or subsidies
- Strained supply chain
- Capital expenditures
- Interest rates
- Currency
- Weather

Identifying stock-specific risks helps an investor evaluate the relative risk and reward potential of firms within a peer group. Identifying systematic risks helps you make informed decisions about which industries and countries to overweight or underweight.

Step 5: Analyze Valuations and Consensus Expectations

Valuations can be a tricky thing. They *are* tools used to evaluate market sentiment and expectations for firms. They *are not* a foolproof way to see if a stock is "cheap" or "expensive." Valuations are primarily used to compare firms against their peer group (or peer average) or a company's valuation relative to its own history. As mentioned earlier, stocks move not on the expected but on the unexpected. We aim to try and gauge what the consensus expects for a company's future performance and then assess whether that company will perform below, in line with, or above expectations.

Valuations provide little information by themselves in predicting future stock performance. Just because one company's P/E is 20 while another's is 10 doesn't mean you should buy the one at 10 because it's "cheaper." There's likely a reason why one company has a different valuation than another, including things like strategic attributes, earnings expectations, sentiment, stock-specific risks, and management's reputation. The utility of valuations lies in uncovering why a company trades at a premium or discount to peers and determining if current pricing is justified.

There are many different valuation metrics investors use in security analysis. Some of the most popular include:

- P/E—price to earnings
- P/FE—price to forward earnings
- P/B—price to book value
- P/S—price to sales
- P/CF—price to cash flow
- DY—dividend yield
- EV/EBITDA—enterprise value to earnings before interest, taxes, depreciation, and amortization

Once you've compiled the valuations for a peer group, try to estimate why there are relative differences and if they're justified. Is a company's relatively low valuation due to stock-specific risk or low confidence from investors? Is the company's forward P/E relatively high because consensus is wildly optimistic about the stock? For example, a firm's higher valuation may be entirely justified if it has a growth rate greater than its peers. A lower valuation may be warranted for a company facing a challenging operating environment in which it is losing market share. Seeing valuations in this way will help to differentiate firms and spot potential opportunities or risks.

Valuations should be used in combination with previous analysis of a company's fundamentals, strategic attributes, and risks. For example, the following grid shows how an investor could combine an analysis of strategic attributes and valuations to help pick firms.

Stocks with relatively low valuations but attractive strategic attributes may be underappreciated by the market (as shown in the following diagram). Stocks with relatively high valuations but no discernible strategic attributes may be overvalued by the market. Either way, use valuations appropriately and in the context of a larger investment opinion about a stock, not as a panacea for true value.

		Valuation Low	Valuation High
Strategic Attributes	Relatively Attractive	Best	
	Relatively Unattractive		Worst

IMPORTANT QUESTIONS TO ASK

While this chapter's framework can be used to analyze any firm, there are additional factors specific to the Consumer Staples sector that must be considered. The following section provides some of the most important factors and questions to consider when researching firms in the sector. Answers to these questions should help distinguish between firms within a peer group and help identify strategic attributes and stock-specific risks. While there are countless other questions and factors that could and should be asked when researching Consumer Staples firms, these should serve as a good starting point.

Product Mix: Well-positioned firms maintain strong market share positions in a variety of products and in growing categories. How diversified is the firm's revenue base? Is it highly exposed to a single product or end market? How does this compare to competitors? Does the firm produce hard-to-copy goods that are differentiated?

Business Strategy: Has the company recently been acquiring or divesting businesses? If so, what are the drivers behind such activity? If the company is a consolidator, does it have a successful track record of creating positive synergies like increased purchasing power, capacity utilization, and distribution network efficiencies? When it comes to acquisitions, you should also investigate risks such as brand dilution and overpaying. You want to know how long it takes for the average deal to be accretive to the bottom line. If a firm is in divestment mode, what were the catalysts and what is the strategy looking forward? Is it moving into higher growth categories? Is the company a turnaround story? If so, what is the estimated timetable for execution?

Geographic Diversity: How wide is the firm's geographic reach? Does the firm have meaningful exposure to high-growth international markets? Is the firm concentrated in a slow-growth, mature market? Geographic diversification can help smooth earnings trends, as growth in one market can offset weakness in other markets. If a company is expanding internationally, what do margins look like in those markets? What are the capital expenditure requirements to build manufacturing and distribution abroad? What is the ROI (return on investment) and how long is the estimated payoff? For internationally diversified firms, keep in mind that fluctuations in foreign currency values influence the way sales and earnings are reported in US dollars.

Input Costs: What are the firm's primary input costs? How have commodity prices been trending and what impact might they have on the firm's margins? Does the company have pricing power to pass through rising input costs? Does it hedge its commodity exposure? If it does hedge, how effective has it been in the past? Oftentimes, monitoring commodity prices requires also monitoring weather patterns, which can have a large impact on supply levels for many commodities.

Competition and Barriers to Entry: What does the competitive landscape look like? Does the firm operate in a fragmented industry or a concentrated industry? Are there firmly entrenched market share leaders who are insulated from smaller competitors via high barriers to entry? If market share changes rapidly, what prompts those changes historically? Is the industry prone to quick-changing fads or is the landscape slow to change? High barriers to entry typically provide pricing power and reduce competition.

Innovation: New product development is crucial in sustaining healthy long-term organic growth. To analyze innovation potential for the future, you should look foremost at the firm's past track record. How successful has it been in pioneering new products versus peers? Is it an industry leader or a "fast follower?" How much does the firm spend annually on R&D as a percentage of sales? Is it consistent in this expense? Lack of consistent R&D investment can result in slowing future organic growth as new breakthrough products are more difficult to roll out.

Breaking Down Sales Growth: Net sales growth is a positive sign for a business, but as a stock analyst you must determine how top-line sales growth is derived if you are to determine the *quality* of the sales growth. Was the top line influenced primarily by acquisitions or divestitures, or was it organic growth from ongoing operations? You can extrapolate organic growth into the future with more confidence than you can with acquisition-based growth, so it is generally considered a more relevant analytic. After you've broken out organic growth, the next question becomes how was that growth achieved? Was it driven through pricing? Increasing unit volume? Analyze whether the firm is growing primarily through one or the other. While price increases are generally a positive, they can be destructive if they lead to volume deterioration, resulting in market share loss. Ideally, a firm will demonstrate strong volume growth along with pricing power, particularly during periods when input costs are accelerating.

Management: What is management's reputation? Is a seasoned team in place with a strong track record of building the business and adding value to shareholders? Have they executed on stated goals and met their guidance to the Street? What has management turnover looked like? Does the firm promote from within or look outside the company for its senior leadership? What is management's policy relative to free cash flow management—are they buying back shares, increasing dividends, or reinvesting in the business? Some executive teams are particularly adept at containing costs, while others are known experts at facilitating new product development and managing expansion. Investigate what management's perceived strengths and weaknesses are, and evaluate whether the right people are at the helm to lead the company in a positive direction.

Brand Equity: A well-respected brand gives a firm the ability to price its product above the competition, deflect substitution effects, and deliver superior profits to investors. People form their self-identities partially based on the brands they buy, attaching particular emotions to products they put *on* or *in* their bodies. This is why branding plays a huge role in the Food, Beverage, and Personal Products categories.

Is the brand highly recognizable? Is it held in high or low regard? What are the firm's strategies in promoting the brand? Have advertising campaigns surrounding key products coincided with increased revenue and market share?

Sales Relationships & Distribution: How does the firm's distribution platform compare to the rest of the industry? If you're looking at a consumer products company, is it able to get shelf space and favorable pricing from retailers? Does it have any type of unique relationships in place with partners? Does the firm have an internal sales force or rely on a third party? Are there any cost advantages or disadvantages to its approach?

Regulation: How are the firm's operations affected by regulation? Does the firm currently operate in a favorable regulatory environment? How might that change? With ever-present concerns around food and beverage safety, the regulatory environment is particularly important to food and beverage companies. Monitor whether the firm you are looking at has incurred recalls of any sort as a result of government or safety group investigations.

Legislation: Are there any legislative risks? These can include royalties, windfall taxes, environmental legislation, price caps, labor laws, subsidies, export taxes, tariffs, and the nationalization of assets. Regional trade agreements are particularly significant in distinguishing market access for a wide variety of Consumer Staples goods.

Trade Up/Trade Down: When disposable income is rising, consumers demonstrate a propensity to trade up in brand quality, usually resulting in increased sales of higher margin products for consumer goods firms. When disposable income is constricted, consumers tend to trade down to private label brands to save money. Is the firm you are researching susceptible to trade up or trade down in the near term? Does it have a private label presence or a stratified price tier among its products that can capture a trade-down effect?

Margins: Are margins growing or shrinking? Why are they growing or shrinking? Has the company historically offset higher costs with higher prices? How do its margins compare to peers? Beware of firms who make uncharacteristic cuts to their advertising budgets—this is a common tactic to smooth short-term earnings that can have negative long-term implications. Expense items should be studied individually and carefully via the income statement. Line items such as selling, general, and administrative (SG&A) and R&D costs should be analyzed in relation to industry norms.

Margins are particularly important in an environment with rising raw material prices. The more commoditized the firm's end market, the less pricing power it typically controls, which can lead to negative earnings during periods of sharply rising input costs. Conversely, strong brand equity and uniquely differentiated products facilitate pricing power, which can stabilize margins during periods of inflation.

SG&A Efficiency: Cost reductions on the SG&A line are a common way firms try to keep the bottom line moving in a favorable direction. There are several productivity metrics you can use to analyze which firms have the most opportunity to improve their efficiency.

What is the firm's *sales-per-employee* ratio? If the ratio is high compared to peers, you're looking at a lean organization. If it is low, perhaps there are opportunities for management to consolidate the operation that would be accretive to earnings. You can find approximations of headcount on most companies' websites or in their filings and will most likely have to compute this ratio manually since it isn't widely reported.

Another productivity metric you can manually calculate that helps assess operational efficiency is the *non-strategic SG&A costs to sales* ratio. To compute this ratio, start by breaking out shipping and handling costs from SG&A (provided they are individually reported). Then strip out R&D, advertising, and promotional spending, and compare your final figure to sales. This analysis will help estimate non-strategic SG&A costs that could probably be cut without meaningfully sacrificing future sales. A lower ratio is preferable here, and the ratio is most useful when comparing firms with similar business models.

Financial Strength: Does the company have enough cash to operate the business well into the future? Compare the firm's interest costs with the amount of operating cash flow the business generates (*interest coverage ratio*). Will the firm require additional funds in the future to expand its operation? If so, is there capacity to take on more debt or would the firm have to engage in an equity offering that may dilute existing shareholders? You can investigate financial health by comparing balance sheet financial ratios to peers. Ratios such as long-term debt to shareholders' equity and the current ratio can be used to assess a firm's capitalization structure and level of liquidity. Comparing credit ratings to peers is another tool at your disposal. The primary credit agencies include Standard & Poor's, Moody's, and Fitch.

Recall debt isn't necessarily a bad thing when defining financial strength—many firms generate an excellent return on borrowed funds. Understanding the capital structure of a firm and its history of generating returns on capital will help you appraise the optimal level of debt.

Chapter Recap

Security analysis is not nearly as complicated as it seems. In the top-down investment process, stocks are essentially tools we use to take advantage of opportunities we identify in higher level themes. Once an attractive segment of the market is identified, we attempt to find firms most likely to outperform their peers by identifying firms with strategic attributes. While the five-step security selection process is just one of many ways to research firms, it is an effective framework for selecting securities within the top-down process.

Don't limit yourself to the questions provided in this chapter when researching Consumer Staples firms— they are just some tools to help you distinguish between firms. The more questions you ask, the better your analysis will be.

- Stock selection, the third and final step in the top-down investment process, attempts to identify securities that will benefit from our high-level portfolio themes.
- Ultimately, stock selection attempts to spot opportunities not currently discounted into prices.
- To identify firms most likely to outperform their peer group, we must find firms that possess competitive advantages (aka strategic attributes).
- A five-step security selection process can be used as a framework to research firms.
- Firms within each industry have specific characteristics and strategies separating potential winners from losers. Asking the right questions can help identify those features.

9

CONSUMERIZE YOUR PORTFOLIO—INVESTING STRATEGIES

In this final chapter, we'll discuss various Consumer Staples investment strategies you can use building on the knowledge in this book. The strategies include:

- Playing the market cycle
- Playing style shifts
- Developing new categorizations

While the strategies presented here are by no means comprehensive, they provide a good starting point for constructing a portfolio that can increase your likelihood of outperforming a Consumer Staples benchmark. They should also help spur some investment strategy ideas of your own. After all, building your own unique framework of investment strategies is the primary way you can discover information few others have discovered yet. And that's what astute investing is all about.

STRATEGY 1: PLAYING THE MARKET CYCLE

Top-down strategists pay particular attention to where they think they are in the market cycle, remaining active in their asset allocation decisions. Market cycles vary in duration and magnitude, so the most important question to ask at any point is: What's the appropriate positioning on a forward-looking basis in terms of asset class, relative to your chosen benchmark? By and large, for most long-term investors, this is a question of whether you should be fully equitized relative to the benchmark, partially equitized, or mostly defensive by holding cash and/or bonds or taking other measures to reduce market-like volatility.

After determining the percentage of equity exposure, the next consideration is sub-asset-allocation decisions like country and sector preferences. Based on these, you can overweight and underweight select categories to target excess return. Determining aggregate country and sector exposures easily warrants another book, but in this chapter we can offer clues to help determine what kind of Consumer Staples sector rotation strategies you can deploy at different points in the market cycle.

Consider what we've already covered in this book. Consumer Staples has historically tended to be one of the most defensive sectors. This may make it an appropriate sector bet should you forecast extended negative stock market performance (like a bear market).

Table 9.1 illustrates sector performance before, during, and after the bear market that started in 2000. While one market cycle doesn't make a trend, we have observed earlier cycles and found similar sector leadership patterns as those transpiring from 2000 to 2002.

As Table 9.1 shows, Consumer Staples was the worst performing sector in the final year of the bull market, producing a –26.9 percent return while the broad market gained 15.0 percent. Historically, it's generally been best to be underweight less economically sensitive categories like Consumer Staples and Health Care in the late stages of a bull market, since they typically underperform more economically sensitive categories like Technology, Energy, and Industrials.

Table 9.1   Sector Performance Before, During, and After the
2000–2002 Bear Market, Average Return

Sector	12M Up to Peak	During Bear	3M Off Bottom	6M Off Bottom	12M Off Bottom	18M Off Bottom
Technology	94.0%	−82.4%	38.9%	33.1%	76.1%	78.1%
S&P 500	15.0%	−49.1%	19.6%	13.4%	32.5%	43.0%
Industrials	8.7%	−38.1%	19.1%	12.4%	34.6%	42.5%
Energy	6.2%	−18.5%	11.1%	8.9%	16.1%	37.1%
Telecom	5.9%	−74.1%	49.1%	18.8%	24.2%	40.6%
Consumer Discretionary	2.1%	−41.2%	12.1%	11.3%	35.3%	45.2%
Utilities	−0.4%	−47.7%	36.2%	22.2%	42.8%	57.5%
Financials	−6.4%	−25.2%	26.4%	17.6%	40.1%	57.4%
Materials	−7.0%	−24.8%	24.7%	13.8%	36.4%	51.6%
Health Care	−16.7%	−6.9%	8.5%	7.4%	11.4%	17.1%
Consumer Staples	−26.9%	24.2%	1.1%	−6.3%	2.2%	11.1%

Source: Global Financial Data.

But during bear markets, Consumer Staples has historically delivered superior returns relative to other economically sensitive equity categories. In the bear market period analyzed, Consumer Staples was the only sector to generate a positive return, rising 24 percent while the market overall declined 49 percent. Few are able to time sector rotation strategies perfectly, but being right more than wrong over the course of several bear markets can make a huge difference in long-term relative returns.

Just as it may be a sound strategy to overweight Consumer Staples in anticipation of a bear market, it may be sound to unwind a Staples overweight should you anticipate a bear market bottom. This is because Consumer Staples has historically delivered relatively poorer returns in the period following a true bear market bottom. As demonstrated in Table 9.1, the sector continued to lag the market further into the new bull market, significantly trailing the market average 6, 12, and 18 months after the bear market bottom. As a bear market progresses, it may make sense to actively pare back Staples exposure, which provides capital to overweight other sectors that may deliver stronger relative returns following the bear.

Beta

One of the factors you should consider when navigating market cycles is volatility. Relative volatility is commonly measured by beta. In a bear market, if you can reduce relative volatility, you may experience less downside than the market experiences. In a bull market, volatility can be your friend. In a rising market, increasing portfolio beta may deliver excess return relative to your benchmark. You can play volatility from a sector level, industry level, and individual stock level.

Consumer Staples and Health Care have historically been the two lowest beta sectors, which helps explain their strong bear market relative performance and poor bull market performance. Meanwhile, Technology has historically been a high-beta sector, explaining its poor bear market performance and strong bull market performance.

Beta

Beta is a measure of systematic risk of a security or a portfolio in comparison to the overall market. It is calculated using regression analysis and is indicative of a security's sensitivity to swings in the market. A beta of 1 means the security, or even a whole sector, moves in tandem with the market. A beta of less than 1 means the security or sector is less volatile than the market, while a beta greater than 1 indicates the security or sector is more volatile than the market.

Consumer Staples Industry Leadership During Market Cycles

Beyond broad sector bets, you can make more granular plays by analyzing industry-level performance. Which Consumer Staples industries have historically performed best during bear markets, and which traditionally presented better opportunities in bull markets? Table 9.2 shows industry leadership for S&P 500 Consumer Staples since 1995—as far back as we have comparative industry data.

Table 9.2   Consumer Staples Industry Leadership Since 1995

Market Type	Date	Food & Staples Retailing	Beverages	Food Products	Household Products	Tobacco	Personal Products
Bull	1/1/1995–3/24/2000	121.8%	96.3%	54.7%	124.5%	24.4%	89.1%
Bear	3/24/2000–10/09/2002	–9.3%	26.2%	46.9%	38.9%	102.4%	4.0%
Bull	10/9/2002–10/9/2007	11.5%	43.2%	68.6%	68.9%	222.9%	150.4%

Source: Thomson Datastream.

As Table 9.2 shows, leadership changes come and go among Consumer Staples industries. Once you've determined the overall Staples percentage target for your portfolio, you should next consider which industries might provide the best hunting ground for individual stocks. Each industry has unique drivers that can influence performance, as discussed in Chapter 4. Beyond those specific drivers, also keep in mind certain industries are slightly more economically sensitive than others.

Food & Staples Retailing and Personal Products, for instance, are slightly more discretionary than Food Products or Tobacco. Consumers spend more money in aggregate shopping at grocery stores than they do on any individual Staples product. This makes retailers more economically sensitive than product manufacturers because consumers notice their grocery receipt totals more readily than they think about how much an individual item, like a candy bar, costs. Such awareness makes demand at the retail level slightly more income and price elastic. When compared to other staples like food, demand for personal products like beauty care items is also more economically sensitive since trade down and demand deferral are more frequent with beauty care items when times get tough.

The different layers of elasticity in the various Staples industries are reflected by their beta differences. While all are relatively lower beta and the deviations are small compared to sector differences, the

Table 9.3   Industry Beta

Industries	Beta
Food & Staples Retailing	0.66
Personal Products	0.61
Beverages	0.57
Household Products	0.57
Food Products	0.51
Tobacco	0.50

betas for the sector's more discretionary areas are higher than the least economically sensitive areas. Table 9.3 breaks down industry beta from 1995 through 2008.[1]

When considering which industries to over- and underweight during different periods of the market cycle, consider:

- Industry-specific drivers
- How economically sensitive the industry is relative to others and whether that is ideal depending on how bullish or bearish you are
- Individual stock considerations like those discussed in Chapter 8

STRATEGY 2: PLAYING STYLE SHIFTS

Unlike some other sectors that are uniformly considered one style (e.g., Technology is considered growth, Energy is value), you can find both growth and value in Consumer Staples stocks. This affords the opportunity to implement style-driven strategies within your sector exposure.

A Brief Primer on Style Shifts

Growth and value come in and out of favor over time. Figure 9.1 demonstrates the historical lead/lag relationship between value and growth, using the Russell 1000 Index as a proxy. The chart shows style leadership generally running a number of years before switching.

So what determines whether a stock is classified as growth or value? Definitions vary, but a simple way of looking at it is using valuations.

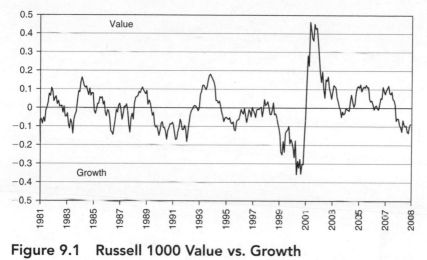

Figure 9.1   Russell 1000 Value vs. Growth
Source: Thomson Datastream.

If a stock trades at a premium to the market (as identified by a bench-mark, such as the S&P 500 or Russell 1000), it usually falls into the growth camp, while stocks that are cheaper relative to the market are considered value. (For more on value versus growth leadership cycles and the reasons behind them, we encourage you to read Ken Fisher's *The Only Three Questions That Count.*)

You can use your style forecasts as a strategy for picking Consumer Staples stocks. For instance, many Food and Tobacco stocks can be classified as value, while most Personal Products companies and Beverages are considered growth. If you have reason to believe value is poised to lead, it's worth checking out companies that tradition-ally trade at low valuations. If you think growth is going to lead, you might be better off looking at firms that usually trade at higher multi-ples than most other Staples stocks.

A word of caution: Historically, one of the worst Consumer Staples investments has been a firm on its way from growth to value territory. This transition most often occurs when growth prospects slow and val-uations begin to contract. One example is Hansen Natural in 2008.

Hansen is known for its Monster Energy drinks, which became popular during the energy drink boom in the mid-2000s. Figure 9.2 shows Hansen's historical stock chart.

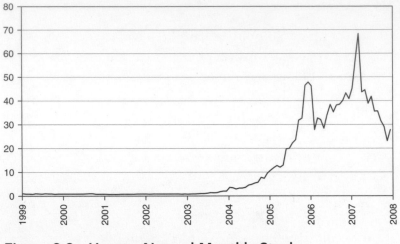

Figure 9.2   Hansen Natural Monthly Stock Performance, December 1998 - August 2008
Source: Thomson Datastream.

After years as a penny stock, times were good for Hansen shareholders from 2004 through most of 2007. In late 2007, however, the energy drink category started to lose some of its pep, and so did the stock. Volumes declined as the "newness" associated with energy drinks died down. Economic slowdown perhaps also made consumers think twice about more discretionary-oriented Staples purchases like energy drinks. Moreover, existing players in the energy drink industry started to feel pressure from the constant stream of new entrants looking to capitalize on the category's above-average growth. As more and more brands hit the market, competition for loyal energy drink consumers increased. These factors created new profitability headwinds for the firm. More impactful to the stock, valuations were knocked down as the growth story became less intriguing.

By mid-September 2008, Hansen traded at a P/E of 14, well off its P/E from a year earlier of 39. The price/sales ratio fell to 2.2 from 5.7, and the stock traded at an Enterprise Value/EBITDA ratio of 7.9 versus 23.6 the prior year (according to Bloomberg Finance L.P.). In a year's time, Hansen transformed from a growth stock to a value stock. Shareholders that held on for the ride paid a hefty price.

Big Versus Small

Just as you can use valuations to separate growth versus value stocks, you can also sort stocks by market capitalization and play size leadership trends. Correctly calling large-cap or small-cap outperformance can help increase portfolio relative performance.

Small-cap stocks generally have higher betas than large caps. This extra degree of volatility historically has helped small caps take off quickly from market bottoms, often delivering relatively superior returns early in market advance. However, small caps have historically tended to sell off sharply following market peaks, frequently underperforming during bear markets.

Big caps historically have delivered relatively superior returns during later periods of market cycles. In very late stages, mega-caps (the biggest of the big) with strong cash balances have historically had superior relative returns. These are times when the great big companies that no one expects to do anything suddenly see a performance burst. (Size leadership trends are also covered in more detail in *The Only Three Questions That Count*).

You can play big/small leadership trends in your individual Consumer Staples stock picks. If you have conviction that big or small will outperform on a forward-looking basis, take that into consideration as a strategy when choosing Staples investments.

STRATEGY 3: DEVELOP NEW CATEGORIZATIONS

The manner in which you categorize things says a lot about how you see the world. If you want to see the market in a unique way, you can develop uncommon ways to categorize stocks. Recall the discussion about Einstein in Chapter 7—Einstein developed an edge on the scientific community because he continually pursued unique ways of interpreting scientific data, which allowed him to see the world through a different lens and led to his breakthrough ideas. Breakthrough ideas can help you outperform the market, and the same principles apply here.

When it comes to Consumer Staples stocks, most of the investor universe breaks the sector down into its industries and sub-industries (as we did in Chapter 4), and stops there. You don't have to be limited by standard conventions, however, and are encouraged not to be. Always be on the lookout for new categories you might be able to separate and sort stocks by.

One unique way to break down the Consumer Staples sector is by operating margin. Premium pricing is more difficult to come by in Consumer Staples than in other sectors like Technology or Health Care, where firms can use patent protection to charge higher prices due to lack of direct competition. Staples industries, by contrast, are intensely competitive. While some Staples firms with strong brands are able to charge more than peers for comparable goods, they lack *vast* product differentiation. This dictates that pricing is always very competitive among peers in this sector. It also makes firms operating in the sector hypersensitive to input costs because they cannot easily pass on cost pressure without suffering competitive consequences.

Based on these sector characteristics, we postulated and tested the theory that Consumer Staples firms possessing higher operating margins should generate superior long-term outperformance when compared to firms operating with thin margins. Higher margins provide more maneuverability in times of rising input costs, while a thin margin structure provides little wiggle room if costs go up, leading to a higher probability of negative earnings.

Figure 9.3 illustrates performance of Consumer Staples stocks within the MSCI World Index.[2] In our study, high- and low-margin groups were defined as the top and bottom thirds, respectively, of the starting universe ranked by operating margin (trailing 4Q EBIT/trailing 4Q sales, rebalanced quarterly). The graph depicts a Total Return Ratio whereby upward movements are indicative of the high-margin basket outperforming the low-margin basket.

As you can see, high-margin Staples consistently outperformed historically. In fact, there were only 2 years when low-margin Staples outperformed in the 13 years studied (1997–1998 and 2002–2003).

How could you use this information? This doesn't necessarily mean you should only buy the highest margin Staples stocks. What we've identified is another singular variable you can consider when selecting

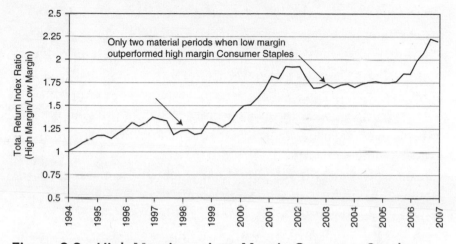

Figure 9.3   High Margin vs. Low Margin Consumer Staples Stocks—Total Return Ratio

Consumer Staples investments along with a host of other variables such as valuation, industry conditions, and strategic attributes. There are no guarantees higher margin Staples firms will continue to generate excess returns versus low-margin firms in the future. However, the evidence is compelling given the causal variables identified. This study also serves as a practical demonstration of how you can use categorization originality to uncover new insights that may not be appreciated by the investment community at large. Play around and test your own innovative theories, however abstract they may appear at first.

IMPLEMENTING YOUR STRATEGY

Once you have determined your strategy, the final step is execution. There are a few ways to go about implementing your ideas.

If playing stylistic trends (big versus small or growth versus value), you could conduct valuation screens similar to those discussed in Chapter 7. If using a unique categorization strategy to dictate Consumer Staples exposure, you might also use fundamentals to conduct individual stock screens. If simply implementing a sector rotational strategy based on your view of the market cycle, you have a couple different options. First, you could once again run a screen for individual stocks based on pre-defined criteria. Second, you also have the option of buying an exchange traded fund (ETF).

Most ETFs provide market-like exposure by mimicking the performance of an index. They are a great tool for times when you lack unique information to posit an investment thesis. For example, if you have no particular view of the Consumer Staples sector, you may not want to overweight or underweight it. You may be better off being market neutral. Likewise, it wouldn't be prudent to buy any individual Staples stocks if you can't form a substantive thesis for owning them. It can be better in these circumstances to buy a Consumer Staples ETF at whatever the sector weight is in your chosen benchmark. To use a golf analogy, you can think of this as laying up and going for par rather than birdie. You're not going to get ahead, but you're also not going to lose ground by hitting a risky shot you don't have confidence in.

Because ETFs differ, investigate each just as you would a stock. Specifically, identify the core holdings of the ETF and determine whether or not its mandate coincides with your objectives (e.g., is it foreign or domestic focused, does it utilize leverage, is it long or short?). Table 9.4 provides a list of the main Consumer Staples ETFs.

Table 9.4   Consumer Staples ETFs

Name	Ticker
First Trust Consumer Staples Alpha	FXG
iShares Dow Jones US Consumer Goods Sector Index	IYK
iShares S&P Global Consumer Staples Index Fund	KXI
PowerShares Dynamic Consumer Staples	PSL
PowerShares FTSE RAFI Consumer Goods Sector Portfolio	PRFG
ProShares Ultra Consumer Goods	UGE
ProShares UltraShort Consumer Goods	SZK
Rydex S&P Equal Weight Consumer Staples	RHS
SPDR S&P International Consumer Staples Sector	IPS
SPDR Select Sector Fund—Consumer Staples	XLP
Vanguard Consumer Staples	VDC
WisdomTree International Consumer Non-Cyclical Sector Fund	DPN

We've covered a lot in these pages—Consumer Staples basics, drivers, and commonly watched industry fundamentals. But remember, like all sectors, Consumer Staples is dynamic. The drivers and fundamentals vital today may not be tomorrow. Herein lies one of the central benefits of the top-down method—it too is dynamic! The tools you have acquired from this book will allow you to apply a consistent framework to analyze the sector in any environment, however it may change in the future.

Chapter Recap

Now is the time to take the knowledge you have accumulated and put it to use. We have highlighted several strategies you can use to manage your Consumer Staples exposure going forward.

- Understanding and playing the market cycle to your advantage is one of the most important strategies you can use to generate excess return.
- No market cycle is an exact replica of the past, but there are patterns that continually repeat.
- Consumer Staples stocks tend to be one of the premier sector performers during bear markets and usually lag over the course of bull markets.
- Consider the degree of elasticity of each Consumer Staples industry when navigating the market cycle.
- Play style shifts to your advantage when possible in your Consumer Staples investments. Pay particular attention to big versus small and growth versus value leadership trends and learn how to parlay trend shifts into the individual stocks you buy.
- Always beware of a Consumer Staples fad stock showing signs of moving from growth to value.
- Experiment with new categorization techniques that you can use to group stocks.
- Higher margin Consumer Staples have demonstrated a stronger ability to weather input cost shocks and have outperformed low-margin Consumer Staples over time.
- You can implement your Consumer Staples sector strategy either through individual stocks or a variety of exchange traded funds.

Appendix
Consumer Staples Sector Resources

While not exhaustive, the websites and publications in the following list are helpful resources to follow economic and sector developments. For those who are time strapped, most major stories relevant to the Consumer Staples sector are covered daily in the *Wall Street Journal*. For those who want more detailed news and statistics, we have broken down many of the sector's premier resources into three categories based on our perception of their usefulness.

Best
- SmartBriefs–Consumer Packaged Goods Publications (http://www.smartbrief.com/news/cpg)
- Beverage World (www.beverageworld.com)
- Chain Drug Review (www.chaindrugreview.com)
- MMR (www.massmarketretailers.com)
- Meat & Poultry (www.meatpoultry.com)
- National Agricultural Statistics Service (www.nass.usda.gov/index.asp)
- Food Processing (www.foodprocessing.com)
- Brandweek (www.brandweek.com)
- Supermarket News (supermarketnews.com)

- Bureau of Economic Analysis (www.bea.gov)
- Bureau of Labor Statistics (www.bls.gov)

Occasionally Useful

- Advertising Age (www.adage.com)
- Agricultural Outlook (www.ers.usda.gov)
- Modern Brewery Age (www.breweryage.com)
- The Beer Institute (www.beerinstitute.org)
- Distilled Spirits Council of the United States (www.discus.org)
- www.tobacco.org
- www.beverageonline.com
- Nonwovens Industry (www.nonwovens-industry.com)
- DSN Retailing Today (www.dsnretailingtoday.com)
- The American Pet Products Manufacturers Association (www .appma.org)
- Drug Store News (www.drugstorenews.com)
- Consumer Product Safety Commission (www.cpsc.gov)
- Federal Trade Commission (www.ftc.gov)
- US Department of Commerce (www.commerce.gov)
- AgLetter (www.chicagofed.org/economic_research_and_data/ ag_conditions.cfm)
- Milling & Banking news (www.bakingbusiness.com/mbn)
- International Dairy Foods Association (www.idfa.org)
- National Grain & Feed Association (www.ngfa.org)
- Progressive Grocer (www.progressivegrocer.com)
- Prepared Foods (www.preparedfoods.com)
- Grocery Manufacturers of America (www.gmabrands.com)
- Food and Agriculture Organization of the United Nations (www.fao.org)
- Agricultural Network Information Center (www.agnic.org/ news)
- Beverage Marketing Corp. (www.beveragemarketing.com)
- The Food Institute (www.foodinstitute.com)
- FoodProductionDaily (www.foodproductiondaily.com)

- Food Marketing Institute (www.fmi.org)
- Beverage Industry (www.bevindustry.com)

Less Frequently Useful

- Beer Marketer's Insights (www.beerinsights.com)
- IMPACT (www.winespectator.com)
- Tobacco Reporter (www.tobaccoreporter.com)
- Campaign for Tobacco-Free Kids (www.tobaccofreekids.org)
- The Wine Institute (http://www.wineinstitute.org)
- Bureau of ATF (www.atf.gov)
- US FDA (www.fda.gov)
- www.taxadmin.gov
- WWD (www.wwd.com)
- Happi (www.happi.com)
- The Soup and Detergent Association (www.cleaning101.com)
- The Personal Care Products Council (www.personalcarecouncil
  .org)
- Organic and Sustainable Industry Standards (www.oasisseal
  .org)
- The Fragrance Foundation (www.fragrance.org)
- Information Resources Inc. (www.infores.com)
- National Cattlemen's Beef Association (www.beef.org)
- Organic Trade Association (www.ota.com)
- National Pork Board (www.porkboard.org)
- National Confectioners Association (www.candyusa.org)
- National Soft Drink Association (www.ameribev.org)
- Datamonitor plc (www.datamonitor.com, www.food-business-review.com, www.drinks-business-review.com)
- Chain Store Age (www.chainstoreage.com)
- Private Label Manufacturers Association (www.plma.com)

Potentially Useful, But Not Free/Easily Accessible

- Amber Waves (www.ers.usda.gov/AmberWaves)
- Handbook Advance (www.beveragehandbooks.com)

- Tobacco Merchants Association of the United States (www .tma.org)
- Just-drinks (www.just-drinks.com)
- Population Reference Bureau (www.prb.org)
- Beverage Digest (www.beverage-digest.com)
- Packaged Facts (www.packagedfacts.com)

Notes

CHAPTER 1: CONSUMER STAPLES BASICS

1. MSCI. The MSCI information may only be used for your internal use, may not be reproduced or redisseminated in any form and may not be used to create any financial instruments or products or any indices. The MSCI information is provided on an "as is" basis and the user of this information assumes the entire risk of any use made of this information. MSCI, each of its affiliates, and each other person involved in or related to compiling, computing, or creating any MSCI information (collectively, the "MSCI Parties") expressly disclaims all warranties (including, without limitation, any warranties of originality, accuracy, completeness, timeliness, non-infringement, merchantability, and fitness for a particular purpose) with respect to this information. Without limiting any of the foregoing, in no event shall any MSCI Party have any liability for any direct, indirect, special, incidental, punitive, consequential (including, without limitation, lost profits), or any other damages.
2. Ibid.
3. See note 1.
4. Ibid.

5. Ibid.
6. Jeremy Siegel, *The Future For Investors*, (Random House Publishing: 2005), 34.
7. Ibid, 36.

CHAPTER 2: HISTORY OF CONSUMERISM IN AMERICA

1. "The Consumer Revolution," Colonial Williamsburg Foundation, http://www   .history.org/history/teaching/enewsletter/volume5/december06/consumer_rev.cfm (accessed September 16, 2008).
2. Joyce Berry, "Three Rivers," http://www.fortklock.com/cosmetic-shygiene.htm (accessed September 16, 2008).
3. Food Timeline, Candies, http://www.foodtimeline.org/foodcandy.html#early americancandy (accessed October 22, 2008).
4. Food Timeline, Colonial America & 17th/18th Century France, http://www.foodtimeline.org/foodcolonial.html#colonialmealtimes (accessed October 22, 2008).
5. See note 1.
6. "American Advertising: A Brief History," History Matters, http://historymatters.gmu.edu/mse/ads/amadv.html (accessed September 16, 2008).
7. Ibid.
8. Ibid.
9. Ellis Hawley, *The Great War and the Search for a Modern Order*, (Waveland Press: 1997); The Library of Congress, "The Prosperity of the Coolidge Era," http://memory.loc.gov/ammem/coolhtml/ccpres01.html (accessed September 16, 2008).
10. J. Bradford DeLong, "Slouching Towards Utopia?: The Economic History of the Twentieth Century," (February 1997), http://econ161.berkeley.edu/tceh/Slouch_roaring13.html (accessed October 22, 2008).
11. International Council of Shopping Centers, "A Brief History of Shopping Centers," (June 2000) http://www.icsc.org/srch/about/

impactofshoppingcenters/briefhistory.html (accessed September 16, 2008).

12. Library of Congress.

13. Ibid.

14. Douglas E. Bowers, "Cooking Trends Echo Changing Roles of Women," Economic Research Service, USDA (January–April 2000), http://www.ers.usda.gov/publications/foodreview/jan2000/frjan2000d.pdf (accessed September 16, 2008).

15. John M. McCann, "The Changing Nature of Consumer Goods Marketing & Sales," Duke University (March 10, 1995), http://www.duke.edu/~mccann/cpg/cg-chg.htm (accessed September 16, 2008).

16. Ibid.

17. Ibid.

18. Ibid.

CHAPTER 3: CONSUMER STAPLES SECTOR DRIVERS

1. Bernard Baumohl, *The Secrets of Economic Indicators*, (Wharton School Publishing: 2005), 104.

2. Coca-Cola 2007 Annual Report.

3. See note 1, 256.

4. Peter Navarro, *If It's Raining in Brazil, Buy Starbucks*, (McGraw-Hill: 2002), 202.

5. Tax Facts History, http://www.nocigtax.com/tax-facts/history (accessed September 16, 2008).

CHAPTER 4: CONSUMER STAPLES SECTOR BREAKDOWN

1. Thomson Datastream, as of December 31, 2007; MSCI. The MSCI information may only be used for your internal use, may not be reproduced or redisseminated in any form, and may not be used to create any financial instruments or products or any

indices. The MSCI information is provided on an "as is" basis and the user of this information assumes the entire risk of any use made of this information. MSCI, each of its affiliates, and each other person involved in or related to compiling, computing, or creating any MSCI information (collectively, the "MSCI Parties") expressly disclaims all warranties (including, without limitation, any warranties of originality, accuracy, completeness, timeliness, non-infringement, merchantability, and fitness for a particular purpose) with respect to this information. Without limiting any of the foregoing, in no event shall any MSCI Party have any liability for any direct, indirect, special, incidental, punitive, consequential (including, without limitation, lost profits), or any other damages.

2. Bloomberg Finance L.P., July 31, 2008.

3. Morningstar, Archer Daniels Midland Corporation Company Profile, http://quote.morningstar.com/Quote/Quote.aspx?ticker=adm (accessed October 23, 2008).

4. William A. Roberts, Jr, "The Hispanic Influence," PreparedFoods (February 1, 2008), http://www.preparedfoods.com/Articles/Feature_Article/BNP_GUID_9-5-2006_A_10000000000000254651 (accessed September 16, 2008).

5. "Industry Overview: Agriculture Crop Production," Hoovers, http://www.hoovers.com/agriculture-crop-production/--ID__35--/free-ind-fr-profile-basic.xhtml (accessed October 23, 2008).

6. "Biofuel Production Boosts Food Prices by 75%, Report Suggests," CBC News, http://www.cbc.ca/world/story/2008/07/04/biofuel-food.html?ref=rss (accessed October 23, 2008).

7. Paul C. Westcott, "U.S. Ethanol Expansion Driving Changes Throughout the Agricultural Sector," United States Department of Agriculture (September 2007), http://www.ers.usda.gov/AmberWaves/September07/Features/Ethanol.htm (accessed June 25, 2008); Ephraim Leibtag, "Corn Prices Near Record High, But What About Food Costs?" United States Department of Agriculture (February 2008), http://www.ers.usda.gov/AmberWaves/February08/Features/

CornPrices.htm (accessed June 25, 2008); "Agrium: Transformation & Growth," (February 2008) http://www.agrium.com/uploads/Morgan_Stanley_08.pdf (accessed June 25, 2008).

8. Thomson Datastream, as of December 31, 2007.

9. Bloomberg Finance L.P, July 31, 2008.

10. *Beverage Digest.*

11. "Beer Consumption in China—Some Figures," Avenue Vine (September 4, 2006), http://www.avenuevine.com/archives/001778.html (accessed October 23, 2008).

12. Standard & Poor's Industry Surveys: Alcoholic Beverages & Tobacco.

13. Ibid.

14. Field Maloney, "Beer in the Headlights," *Slate* (May 30, 2007), http://www.slate.com/id/2167292 (accessed September 23, 2008).

15. See note 16.

16. Jenny Wiggins, "Thirst To Be First: Race For a Global Lead in Beer," *Financial Times* (July 23, 2008), http://www.ft.com/cms/s/0/8b4b2236-58d0-11dd-a093-000077b07658.html?nclick_check=1 (accessed September 23, 2008).

17. Bloomberg Finance L.P., July 31, 2008.

18. See note 16.

19. Bloomberg Finance L.P.

20. "Master Settlement Agreement," State of California Department of Justice, Office of the Attorney General, http://ag.ca.gov/tobacco/msa.php (accessed October 23, 2008).

21. Thomson Datastream, as of December 31, 2007.

22. Bloomberg Finance L.P., July 31, 2008.

23. "The Legacy That Got Left on the Shelf," *Economist* (January 31, 2008), http://www.economist.com/displaystory.cfm?story_id=10601552 (accessed September 23, 2008).

24. Thomson Datastream, as of December 31, 2007.

25. Progressive Grocer 74th Annual Report of the Grocery Industry, April 2007, 44.

26. Bloomberg Finance L.P., July 31, 2008.

27. David Faber, CNBC's "The Age of Wal-Mart: Inside America's Most Powerful Company," documentary special report.

28. Ibid.

29. Standard & Poor's Industry Surveys: Supermarkets & Drugstores, January 24, 2008.

30. Ibid.

CHAPTER 5: CHALLENGES IN THE CONSUMER STAPLES SECTOR

1. Darren Rovell, *First in Thirst: How Gatorade Turned the Science of Sweat Into a Cultural Phenomenon,* (AMACOM Books: 2006), 153.

2. Ibid.

3. Ibid., 98.

4. Barry Winer with Professor Sydney Finkelstein, "Tuck School of Business at Dartmouth Case Study: Quaker Oats and Snapple," Tuck School of Business at Dartmouth (1996), http://mba.tuck.dartmouth.edu/pdf/2002-1-0041.pdf (accessed September 23, 2008).

5. John Deighton, "How Snapple Got Its Juice Back," Harvard Business Review (January 2002).

6. See note 4.

7. Ibid.

8. See note 5.

9. "Triarc to Sell Snapple Beverage Group to Cadbury Schweppes; Enterprise Value of $1.45 Billion," BevNet (September 18, 2000), http://www.bevnet.com/news/2000/09-18-2000-snapple.asp (accessed September 23, 2008).

10. Management interview of Clayton Daley, Vice Chairman and Chief Financial Officer of Procter & Gamble, conducted 5/15/2008 in Woodside, California.

11. Matt Andrejczak, "Pilgrim's Pride to Idle Plants, Cut More Jobs," MarketWatch (August 11, 2008), http://www.marketwatch.com/

news/story/pilgrims-pride-sheds-more-jobs/story.aspx?guid=
%7BC10CA644-C272-4B60-A7E3-D5991677B622%
7D&dist=msr_1 (accessed September 23, 2008).

CHAPTER 6: CONSUMER STAPLES IN EMERGING
MARKETS

1. Antoine van Agtmael, *The Emerging Markets Century: How a New Breed of World-Class Companies Is Overtaking the World*, (Free Press, 2007), 11.
2. CK Prahalad, *The Fortune at the Bottom of the Pyramid: Eradicating Poverty through Profits*, (Wharton School Publishing, 2006), 24.
3. Ibid, 33.
4. "The Legacy that Got Left on the Shelf," *Economist* (January 31, 2008), http://www.economist.com/displaystory.cfm?story_id=10601552 (accessed September 23, 2008).
5. See note 2, 44.
6. Ibid.
7. Ibid.
8. Ibid., 51.
9. Ibid., 40.
10. Julie Jargon, "Kraft Reformulates Oreo, Scores in China," *Wall Street Journal* (May 1, 2008), http://online.wsj.com/public/article_print/SB120958152962857053.html (accessed September 23, 2008).

CHAPTER 7: THE TOP-DOWN METHOD

1. Matthew Kalman, "Einstein Letters Reveal a Turmoil Beyond Science," *Boston Globe* (July 11, 2006), http://www.boston.com/news/world/middleeast/articles/2006/07/11/einstein_letters_reveal_a_turmoil_beyond_science/ (accessed May 9, 2008).
2. Berkshire Hathaway 2005 Annual Report.

3. Michael Michalko, "Combinatory Play," Creative Thinking, http://www.creativethinking.net/DT10_CombinatoryPlay.htm?Entry=Good (accessed May 9, 2008).

4. Gary P. Brinson, Brian D. Singer, and Gilbert L. Beebower, "Determinants of Portfolio Performance II: An Update," The Financial Analysts Journal 47 (1991) 3.

5. MSCI. The MSCI information may only be used for your internal use, may not be reproduced or redisseminated in any form, and may not be used to create any financial instruments or products or any indices. The MSCI information is provided on an "as is" basis and the user of this information assumes the entire risk of any use made of this information. MSCI, each of its affiliates, and each other person involved in or related to compiling, computing, or creating any MSCI information (collectively, the "MSCI Parties") expressly disclaims all warranties (including, without limitation, any warranties of originality, accuracy, completeness, timeliness, non-infringement, merchantability, and fitness for a particular purpose) with respect to this information. Without limiting any of the foregoing, in no event shall any MSCI Party have any liability for any direct, indirect, special, incidental, punitive, consequential (including, without limitation, lost profits), or any other damages.

6. Ibid.

7. Ibid.

8. Ibid.

9. Ibid.

10. Ibid.

CHAPTER 9: CONSUMERIZE YOUR PORTFOLIO— INVESTING STRATEGIES

1. Beta was calculated based on daily performance for the period of December 30, 1994 to September 5, 2008.

2. This study was performed using Clarifi statistical software and the
   WorldScope database with the following data:

   -The starting universe reflected Consumer Staples companies
   within the largest 2000 stocks by market cap among the MSCI
   World Index constituent countries, rebalanced quarterly.

   -High- and low-margin buckets were defined as the top and bottom thirds, respectively, of the starting universe ranked by operating margin (trailing 4Q EBIT/trailing 4Q sales, rebalanced
   quarterly).

About the Authors

Michael Cannivet (San Mateo, California) is the Consumer Staples Research Analyst at Fisher Investments. He is also a contributing columnist for MarketMinder.com. Michael graduated from Georgetown University with a bachelor's degree in Government. Originally from Chicago, he currently resides in the Bay Area with his wife, Jennifer.

Andrew S. Teufel (San Francisco, California) has been a member of Fisher Investments research staff since 1995 and is currently Co-President and Director of Research. Prior to joining the firm, he worked at Bear Stearns as a corporate finance analyst. He is a graduate of the University of California at Berkeley, and has lectured at the Haas School of Business on topics in investment management. Andrew has conducted hundreds of investment seminars and educational workshops throughout the US and the United Kingdom. He also serves as Editor-in-Chief of MarketMinder.com.

Index